Junior Cycle Home Economics

# SKILLS for Life

## Skills & Learning Log

**Carmel Enright**

**Maureen Flynn**

**Consultant Reviewer:**
Maria Hickey

FOLENS

First published in 2018 by Folens Publishers
Hibernian Industrial Estate, Greenhills Road, Tallaght, Dublin 24

© Carmel Enright and Maureen Flynn 2018

**Illustrations:** ODI

ISBN 978-1-78090-894-6

**Photograph acknowledgements**

Bord Bia, iStock, Shutterstock

The publisher has made every effort to contact all copyright holders but if any have been
overlooked, we will be pleased to make any necessary arrangements.

Any links or references to external websites should not be construed as an endorsement by Folens
of the content or views of these websites.

# Contents

Preface .. .. … … … … … … … … … … … … … … … … … … … … … … … .. iv

## STRAND 1 Food, health and culinary skills

1 Food choices.. .. … … … … … … … … … … … … … … … … … … .. 1

2 Nutrition .. .. … … … … … … … … … … … … … … … … … .. 4

3 Balanced eating … … … … … … … … … … … … … … … … .. .. .12

4 Special diets … … … … … … … … … … … … … … … … … .. .21

5 Meal planning .. … … … … … … … … … … … … … … … … .. .27

6 Food safety and hygiene. … … … … … … … … … … … … … .33

7 Food preparation … … … … … … … … … … … … … … … … .38

8 Cooking food . … … … … … … … … … … … … … … … … . .. .42

9 Meat, fish and protein alternatives .. … … … … … … … … … .. .48

10 Milk, cheese and eggs .. … … … … … … … … … … … … … .57

11 Vegetables, fruit and cereals … … … … … … … … … … … … .67

12 Home baking . … … … … … … … … … … … … … … … . .. .76

13 Food shopping.. … … … … … … … … … … … … … … … … .. .81

14 Food sustainability . … … … … … … … … … … … … … … .. .88

15 Digestion.. … … … … … … … … … … … … … … … … … .94

16 Recipes and culinary skills . … … … … … … … … … … … .. .98

17 Classroom-based assessment 2 and the practical exam. .. … … … … .. ..102

## STRAND 2 Responsible family living

18 The family .. … … … … … … … … … … … … … … … … .. ..106

19 Health and wellbeing … … … … … … … … … … … … … … .. ..111

20 The consumer .. … … … … … … … … … … … … … … … .. ..120

21 Decision-making.. .. … … … … … … … … … … … … … … .. ..129

22 Design in the home .. … … … … … … … … … … … … … … .. ..136

23 Technology in the home . … … … … … … … … … … … … … .. ..144

24 Sustainable and responsible living … … … … … … … … … … … .. ..149

## STRAND 3 Textiles and craft

25 Textile trends and choices. … … … … … … … … … … … … .. ..155

26 Sewing skills … … … … … … … … … … … … … … … … .. ..162

27 Fabric embellishment .. … … … … … … … … … … … … … .. ..168

28 Sustainability in textiles … … … … … … … … … … … … … … .. ..171

29 Textile care.. .. … … … … … … … … … … … … … … … .. ..174

30 Classroom-based assessment 1: Creative textiles .. … … … … … … … … .. ..179

# Preface

The *Skills and Learning Log* is designed to encourage self-directed learning. It aims to engage students in the development of the skills involved in becoming competent consumers, responsible, caring citizens and active members of their communities. Included are:

- A selection of fill-in questions, of varying difficulty, which encourage higher order thinking. The language used reflects the glossary of action verbs in the Home Economics specification.

- Anagrams, word searches and crosswords provide opportunities for students to engage in collaborative learning.

- Case studies help to develop communication and decision-making skills.

- Sample tasks for First, Second and Third Years help to develop practical culinary skills, and a self-assessment sheet allows students to evaluate their practical preparation and class work.

- Templates for comparing and evaluating a range of products help students to develop their consumer competency.

- A range of research and investigations in the 'Over to you' section encourages student-directed, discovery learning, often through using IT.

- A 'Learning checklist' at the end of each chapter and a 'Key skills checklist' at the end of each strand allow students to monitor their own learning.

# Food choices

1. State three reasons why we eat food.

   (a) _food is a source of nourishment_

   (b) _food appeals to ~~ous~~ our senses_

   (c) _food is a way of celebrating_

2. The functions of food are:

   (a) To supply _heat_ and _energy_

   (b) For growth and _repair_

   (c) To protect against _disease_

3. Identify four factors that affect our choice of food.

   (a) _nutritional knowledge_

   (b) _cost_

   (c) _culture_

   (d) _family / lifestyle_

4. How does nutritional knowledge help when making food choices?

   _nutritional knowledge helps people to make good food choices and stay healthy_

5. Explain one way in which advertising may influence which foods people choose.

   _advertisement makes us aware of new food products and tries to make people buy these products._

6. Culture might affect a person's food choices. Give one example.

   _certain foods are associated with different cultures, for example pasta is a staple food in Italy_

7. Why is rice a staple food in China?

   _rice is plentiful in China and therefore is cheaper_

8. Explain why buying local food is a sustainable choice.

   _buying local food is a sustainable choice as less energy is used to transport it_

9. Identify one example of an ethical food choice. _buying Fairtrade foods such as tea and coffee_

10. Suggest two advantages of Fairtrade shopping.

    (a) _Fairtrade ensures that farmers are paid a fair price for their goods_

    (b) _Fairtrade aims to improve working conditions for workers in poorer countries_

11. The five senses are:

    (a) _smell_

    (b) _Sight_

    (c) _taste_

    (d) _hearing_

    (e) _touch_

12. Give a brief account of how any one sense affects food choice.

    _taste influences our enjoyment of food most as we all have likes and_
    _dislikes in relation to flavours of food_

13. Mark the position of the taste buds on the tongue on the picture below.

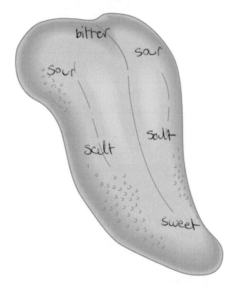

14. Give one example of a food that matches each flavour.

| Sweet | Salty | Sour | Bitter | Umami |
|-------|-------|------|--------|-------|
| honey ~~chocolate~~ | crisps | lemon | dark chocolate | beef |

15. Identify which of your senses detects the following sensory qualities of food.

    (a) Appearance and colour:

    _sight_

    (b) Flavour:

    _taste_

    (c) Texture:

    _touch_

# Over to you 👈

**1.** Match the foods listed in A with the associated country in B.

| A | B | |
|---|---|---|
| 1. Sushi | Italy | 4 |
| 2. Roast beef and Yorkshire pudding | USA | 10 |
| 3. Moussaka | Russia | |
| 4. Pizza | Greece | |
| 5. Paella | Japan | 1 |
| 6. Sweet and sour pork | Spain | 5 |
| 7. Frankfurters | England | |
| 8. Goulash | Germany | 7 |
| 9. Beef stroganoff | Hungary | |
| 10. Hamburgers | China | |

**2.** Set up a taste test of a selection of five different foods. Taste each food and desribe the sensory qualities of the food.

# Learning checklist

| Red: I don't know this. Orange: I need to study this again. Green: Good to go! | 🔴 | 🟠 | 🟢 |
|---|---|---|---|
| I can suggest reasons why we eat food. | | | |
| I can state the functions of food in the body. | | | |
| I can identify and I understand the importance of thinking through my food choices. | | | |
| I understand how the environment is affected by food choices. | | | |
| I appreciate that making ecological food choices is less damaging to the environment. | | | |
| I appreciate what is meant by ethics. | | | |
| I can give examples of ethical food choices and I can imagine how our food choices could affect others. | | | |
| I can appreciate how our senses influence our food choices. | | | |
| I can illustrate the position of taste buds on the tongue. | | | |

**The topic I most enjoyed in this chapter:** _____

**The topic I would like to learn more about:** _____

# 2 Nutrition

## Nutrition

1. Define the following terms.

   (a) Nutrition: _the study of food – its composition and the amounts needed by the body, and its effects on the body_

   (b) Nutrient: _any substance that can be digested and used by the body_

   (c) Wellbeing: _the state of being comfortable, healthy and happy._ mind and body proportions

2. A balanced diet is _a diet containing all of the nutrients in the correct amount for the needs of the body to ensure health and wellbeing._

3. Explain the following terms.

   (a) Sources: _foods where the nutrient is found_

   (b) Functions: _what the nutrient does in the body_ ~~Mind and body~~

4. (a) List the six nutrients.

   (i) _protein_               (ii) _vitamins_

   (iii) _fat_                 (iv) _minerals_

   (v) _carbohydrate_          (vi) _water_

   (b) Name two nutrients under each of the following headings:

   | Macronutrient | Micronutrient |
   | --- | --- |
   | proteins | vitamins |
   | carbohydrates | minerals |

   (c) Distinguish between macronutrients and micronutrients.

   _macronutrients are needed in large amounts and micronutrients are needed in small amounts_

## Protein

1. Protein is composed of the elements _carbon, hydrogen, oxygen and nitrogen_

2. Indicate whether the following statements are true or false:

   | Statement | True | False |
   | --- | --- | --- |
   | The element needed for growth is hydrogen. | | ✓ |
   | The elements in proteins are organised into units called amino acids. | ✓ | |
   | Animal proteins are also referred to as high biological value proteins. | ✓ | |

3. Classify proteins into two groups, and give two examples of each group.

| Class | Examples |
|---|---|
| HBV (High Biological Value) | meat, eggs |
| LBV (Low Biological value) | beans, lentils |

4. Suggest two advantages of using vegetable foods as a source of protein.

(a) _they contain less fat_

_____.

(b) _less land is needed to make plant-based foods than to raise_ _animals._    high in fibre

5. State two functions of protein.

(a) _growth and repair_

(b) _production of hormones, enzymes and antibodies_

# Fats     heat and energy

1. Complete the following sentences:

Fats are also called _lipids_. They are composed of the elements _carbon_,

_hydrogen_ and _oxygen_.

2. Indicate whether the following statements are true or false:

| Statement | True | False |
|---|---|---|
| Fats are composed of amino acids. | ○ | ✓ |
| Vegetable fats are unsaturated fats. | ✓ | ○ |
| Overeating fats may cause obesity. | ✓ | ○ |

3. The functions of fat are:

(a) To provide _heat_ and _energy_.

(b) To prevent _heat_ _loss_.

(c) To protect _delicate_ _organs_, for example _the kidneys_.

4. (a) State a beneficial effect of including unsaturated fats in the diet.

_____some unsaturated fats help reduce cholesterol in the blood_

_____

(b) Identify a beneficial effect of including omega fatty acids in the diet.

_____omega fatty acids are thought to reduce the risk of heart disease_

_omega three helps the brain send_

_omega three increases brain function_

5. What are the dangers to health of eating too much saturated or hydrogenated fat?

eating too much saturated or hydrogenated fat could lead to the build-up of cholesterol in the blood vessels. This can cause high blood pressure, strokes and heart disease.

6. List two ways of reducing fat in the diet.

    (a) replacing ~~fatty~~ e.g crisps fatty snacks with healthier ones with vegetables

    (b) ~~drinking water instead of soft drinks.~~ Choose low fat dairy products    don't deep fry foods; choose healthy cooking methods

# Carbohydrates

1. Complete the following sentences:

    (a) Carbohydrates come from ___plant___ foods only.

    (b) Carbohydrates are made by a process called ___photosynthesis___.

2. Identify two sources of each of the following:

| Class | Sources | |
|---|---|---|
| Sugar | Cakes | ~~sugar~~ biscuits |
| Starch | potatoes | bread |
| Cellulose | vegetables | fruit |

dietary fibre → Cellulose

3. State two functions of carbohydrates.

    (a) heat and energy

    (b) ~~excess~~ extra carbohydrates are stored as ~~fats~~ fat for insulation

4. Indicate whether the following statements are true or false:

| Statement | True | False |
|---|---|---|
| It is recommended that we eat 15 g of cellulose daily. | ○ | ✓ |
| Cellulose aids the movement of food through the digestive system. | ✓ | ○ |
| Too much sugar causes tooth decay. | ✓ | ○ |

5. (a) What is meant by RDA?

    RDA means Recommended ~~daily~~ dietary Allowance/amount

    (b) State the recommended RDA of fibre per day.

    30g

# Vitamins

1. Classify vitamins and give examples.

| Class | Examples |
|---|---|
| fat-soluble vitamins | A, D, E, K |
| water-soluble vitamins | B, C |

2. State one source of each of the following vitamins:

Vitamin A ~~fish~~ carrots

Vitamin B ~~breakfast~~ ~~cereals~~ fish

Vitamin C citrus fruits ✓

Vitamin D sunlight ✓

Vitamin E nuts ✓

Vitamin K ~~blueberries~~ green vegetables

3. Match the vitamin with the appropriate function:

| Vitamin | Function | |
|---|---|---|
| A | Healthy nervous system | vitamin B ✓ |
| B | Prevents rickets | vitamin D ✓ |
| C | Prevents scurvy | vitamin C ✓ |
| D | Growth good eyesight | vitamin A ✓ |

4. Identify a different deficiency disease caused by a low intake of each of the following vitamins:

| Vitamin | Deficiency | |
|---|---|---|
| C | scurvy ✓ | anaemia |
| A | ~~delayed growth~~ | night blindness |
| D | rickets and | osteoporosis |
| K | blood will not clot normally to KLOT the blood ✓ | |

5. Complete the following sentences:

(a) Vitamin D works with calcium to build healthy bones and teeth.

(b) Carotene changes to vitamin A in the body.

**6.** Indicate whether the following statements are true or false:

| Statement | True | False |
|---|---|---|
| If a vitamin is missing from the diet, a deficiency disease may develop. | ✓ | ○ |
| Vitamins can only be obtained from food. | ○ | ✓ |
| B and C are the fat-soluble vitamins. | ○ | ✓ |
| Water-soluble vitamins dissolve in fat. | ○ | ✓ |
| Carotene changes to vitamin A in the body. | ✓ | ○ |
| Liver and kidneys supply vitamin A. | ✓ | ○ |
| Rickets develops from lack of vitamin A. | ○ | ✓ |
| Vitamin D is needed for normal blood clotting. | ○ | ✓ |
| Vitamin C can be made by bacteria in the body. | ○ | ✓ |
| Sunlight is a good source of vitamin D. | ✓ | ○ |
| Meat is a good source of vitamin C. | ○ | ✓ |
| Beriberi is a bone disease. | ○ | ✓ |
| Night-blindness may be caused by lack of vitamin C. | ○ | ✓ |
| Fruit and vegetables are the best source of vitamin C. | ✓ | ○ |
| Scurvy develops from consuming too much vitamin C. | ○ | ✓ |
| Vitamin B is a water-soluble vitamin. | ✓ | ○ |

# Minerals

vitamin C and iron prevent anemia

**1.** Match the mineral with its function.

| Mineral | Function |
|---|---|
| Calcium | In all body fluids  *Sodium* |
| Iron | Keeps bones and teeth healthy  *Calcium* |
| Sodium | Bone and teeth formation  *Phosphorus* |
| Phosphorus | Healthy blood  *Iron* |

2. State two sources of each of the following minerals.

   (a) Sodium: _sea bacon_ _peanuts_

   (b) Calcium: _milk_ _green vegetables_

   (c) Phosphorus: _eggs_ _cheese_

3. Indicate whether the following statements are true or false:

| Statement | True | False |
| --- | --- | --- |
| Phosphorous works with calcium in the diet. | ✓ | ○ |
| Vitamin D aids the absorption of iron. | | ✓ |
| Anaemia results from lack of iodine. | ○ | ✓ |

4. Identify the condition associated with the following symptoms:

   (a) The bones become thin and fracture easily. _osteoporosis_

   (b) Tiredness, lack of energy and headaches. _anaemia_

## Test yourself

   (a) Minerals are needed in the body in _small_ amounts.

   (b) _tinned_ fish are good sources of calcium.

   (c) _rickets_ is a bone disease that occurs in children.

   (d) Calcium is necessary for healthy _bones_ and _teeth_.

   (e) _Phosphorous_ helps calcium to form teeth and _bones_.

   (f) Iron is necessary to form _haemoglobin_ in the _red blood cells_.

   (g) Lack of iron may cause _anaemia_.

   (h) _Sodium_ is found in all bodily fluids.

   (i) Anaemia can be corrected by a diet rich in _iron_.

# Water

1. Water is composed of the elements _hydrogen_ and _oxygen_.

2. Identify three foods that have a high water content.

   (a) _coffee_    (b) _drinking water_    (c) _fruit_

3. Two functions of water are:

   (a) _carries nutrients and oxygen to the body_    (b) _regulates body temperature_

4. List two properties of pure water.

   (a) _odourless_    (b) _colourless_

# Over to you

1. Solve the following anagrams of nutrient sources.

| Proteins | | | | |
|---|---|---|---|---|
| GEGS | SANBE | TEAM | SIFH | ESECHE |
| | | | | |

| Fats | | | | |
|---|---|---|---|---|
| TUSN | LOIS | MACRE | HEEECS | RETBUT |
| | | | | |

| Carbohydrates | | | | |
|---|---|---|---|---|
| ICER | SATOEPOT | TASAP | DERAB | SITCUISB |
| | | | | |

2. Look at the Food table on pp. 187–9 of your *Skills for Life* textbook. Find out how much protein is found in 100 g/100 ml of the following foods.

| Food | Protein per 100 g/100 ml | Food | Protein per 100 g/100 ml |
|---|---|---|---|
| Whole milk | | Eggs | |
| Baked beans | | Cheddar cheese | |
| Plaice | | Roast chicken | |
| Frozen peas | | Peanuts | |

3. Create and display wall charts of the following:

- Protein foods
- Foods high in fat
- Foods high in fibre
- Foods high in sugar
- Foods high in vitamins and minerals

# Learning checklist

**Red: I don't know this.** Orange**: I need to study this again.** Green: **Good to go!**  ● ● ●

I can define the terms nutrition, nutrient, RDA and GDA.

I appreciate the importance of nutrition and diet in contributing to health and wellbeing.

I can distinguish between macronutrients and micronutrients and I can give examples of both.

I can outline the composition, RDA and functions of protein.

I can classify protein into two groups and I can give examples of protein foods in each group.

I can state the composition, classification, sources and functions of fats.

I understand the dangers of eating too much saturated fat.

I appreciate the benefits of unsaturated fats in the diet.

I can outline the composition, classification, sources and functions of carbohydrate.

I can explain the role of fibre in a healthy diet.

I appreciate too much sugar is not good for you and I can suggest ways of reducing sugar in the diet.

I can classify vitamins into two groups and I can give examples in each group.

I can state sources, functions and effects of deficiency of vitamins A, D, E, K, B and C.

I can list the minerals and give their sources and functions.

I know the effects of a deficiency in these minerals and I can give an account of some deficiency diseases.

I can outline the composition, sources, functions, properties and RDA of water.

I can explain the role of each nutrient in a healthy balanced diet.

**The topic I most enjoyed in this chapter:** _____

**The topic I would like to learn more about:** _____

# 3 Balanced eating

## Energy

1. Define the following terms.

    (a) Energy: _the ability to do work_

    (b) Metabolic rate: _the rate at which we use energy_

    (c) Basal metabolic rate: _the least amount of energy required to keep the body alive_

2. Identify two nutrients that supply the body with energy.

    (a) _carbohydrate_

    (b) _protein_

3. Complete the following:

    (a) 1 gram of protein gives __4__ kcal or __17__ kJ.

    (b) 1 gram of carbohydrate gives __4__ kcal or __17__ kJ.

    (c) 1 gram of fat gives __9__ kcal or __38__ kJ.

4. State two functions of energy.

    (a) _the working of internal organs_

    (b) _maintaining body temperature._

5. State four factors that affect energy requirements.

    (a) _age_

    (b) _size_

    (c) _gender_

    (d) _climate_

6. Define the term 'balanced diet'.

    _a diet containing all the nutrients in the correct amounts for the needs of the body to ensure_
    _health and wellbeing_

7. What proportion of a balanced diet should each of the following nutrients make up?

    (a) Protein: _10 - 35%_

    (b) Fat: _20 - 35%_

    (c) Carbohydrate: _45 - 65%_

**8.** Complete the following using the food pyramid on p. 30 of your textbook.

| | Nutrients supplied | Number of recommended servings |
|---|---|---|
| Vegetables, salad and fruit | | 5 - 7 |
| Wholemeal cereals and breads, potatoes, pasta and rice | | 3 - 5 |
| Milk, yoghurt and cheese | | 3 |
| Meat, poultry, fish, eggs, beans and nuts | | 2 |
| Fats, spreads and oils | | small amounts |
| Top shelf | | not every day |

**9.** State four current healthy eating guidelines.

(a) _wide vareity of foods_

(b) _increase fibre intake_

(c) _choose low-fat milk, cheese & yoghurt_

(d) _choose lean meat and poultry._

**10.** Complete the following sentences:

In a healthy diet reduce s _alt_ , s _ugar_ and saturated _fat_ .

Increase f _ibre_ , w _ater_ and f _ruits_ and v _egetables_ .

**11. (a)** Recommend four guidelines for health and wellbeing.

(i) _eat a healthy balanced diet_

(ii) _get sufficient rest and sleep_

(iii) _maintain good personal hygiene_

(iv) _do not smoke or abuse alchohol or drugs_

**(b)** How much daily exercise is recommended for teenagers?

_60 mins_

# Babies

**1. (a)** Explain the term 'weaning'. *when solid foods such as cereals are introduced to a baby at around 4-6 months*

**(b)** At what stage does this occur? *4 - 6 months*

**2. (a)** What nutrients are introduced into a baby's diet by the addition of the following foods?

| Food | Nutrient |
| --- | --- |
| Cereals | ~~fibre~~ carbohydrate |
| Fruit and vegetables | fibre |

**(b)** Explain why a vitamin D supplement is recommended for children under the age of one year.

*to prevent weak bones*

**3. (a)** Explain why babies are particularly sensitive to food poisoning.

*because they are small it is easier to upset their digestive systems ~~the~~ or give them food poisoning*

**(b)** Identify two hygiene rules that should be followed when preparing baby food.

**(i)** *wash hands before preparing food*

**(ii)** _____

# Children/Adolescents

**1.** Why are these nutrients of particular importance to teenagers?

| Nutrient | Reason |
| --- | --- |
| Protein | for growth |
| Vitamin C | ~~for energy~~ to prevent anaemia |
| Iron | for healthy bones & teeth |
| Calcium | ~~repro~~ to prevent anaemia |

**2.** Suggest two healthy snacks and two unhealthy snacks for children.

**(a)** _____

**(b)** _____

**(c)** _____

**(d)** _____

# Adults

**1. (a)** Identify two benefits of including unsaturated fat in the diet.

    **(i)** reduce cholesterol

    **(ii)** omega fatty acids are associated with improved brain function

**(b)** State the functions and sources of omega fatty acids.

| Functions | Sources |
| --- | --- |
| reduce risk of heart disease | oily fish |
| improve brain ~~fad~~ function | seeds |

**2. (a)** Explain why women more likely to suffer from anaemia than men.

Women are more likely to suffer from anaemia due to the blood loss menstruation,

**(b)** Why are women more likely to suffer from bone disease than men?

Women are more likely to suffer from bone disease than men due to how calcium may be removed

from their bones during the childbearing years.

**3. (a)** Differentiate between sedentary workers and manual workers.

Sedentary workers are office workers and manual workers do manual labour, e.g. farmer.

**(b)** List four nutritious high-energy foods suitable for a manual worker.

    **(i)** porridge

    **(ii)**

    **(iii)**

    **(iv)**

4.  The following is a day's menu for an active man. Rewrite this menu for (a) an inactive woman in a sedentary occupation and (b) for a child.

| Orange juice |
| :---: |
| Porridge |
| Fried bacon, egg, sausage |
| 2 slices of toast |
| Tea |

| Ham and cheese sandwiches |
| :---: |
| Slice of fruitcake |
| Apple |
| Tea |

| Roast chicken |
| :---: |
| Roast potatoes |
| Carrots, peas |
| Gravy |
| Cheesecake, cream |

| **(a) Inactive woman** |
| --- |
|  |

| **(b) Child** |
| --- |
|  |

5. (a) Identify four nutrients of particular importance during pregnancy, giving their functions and possible sources.

| Nutrient | Function | Source |
|---|---|---|
| vitamin A | growth | oily fish, liver, eggs, carrots, peppers |
| vitamin D | healthy bones & teeth | sunlight, oily fish |
| calcium | healthy bones & teeth | milk, cheese, eggs |
| protein | growth and repair | meat, eggs, peas, beans, lentils, nuts, cereals |

(b) Write an informative note on folic acid (see p. 20 of your textbook).

Folic acid can be found in fortified breakfast cereals and wholemeal bread. Folic acid helps prevent neural tube defects. An example of a deficiency disease from lack of folic acid would be a neural tube defect, for example spina bifida in newborn babies.

# The elderly and convalescents

1. (a) Explain why protein is important in the diet of the elderly.

(b) Suggest why the elderly should reduce their consumption of high-energy foods.

2. (a) Identify a deficiency disease associated with the elderly.

Osteoperosis

(b) Explain how this disease might be prevented.

Including vitamins A and D and calcium in the diet.

3. Explain the term 'convalescent'.

Someone who is sick or recovering from an illness.

4.  Explain why the following nutrients are of particular importance to convalescents.

| Nutrient | Reasons |
|----------|---------|
| Water | prevents dehydration |
| Vitamin C | helps return to health and build up resistance |
| Protein | to repair and replace body cells |
| Iron | to prevent the patient from becoming anaemic |

5.  Identify one method of cooking which should be avoided when preparing meals for convalescents.

    _____

    Give a reason for your answer.

    _____

    _____

    _____

    _____

# Over to you

1.  Examine the case study below and answer the questions that follow.

## Case study

Rachel was late for work. She did not have time for breakfast. She rushed to catch the bus.
By break-time she was starving, so she bought a bag of crisps and a bar of chocolate in the shop
across the street. At lunchtime she was not really hungry, so she ate only half of the chicken salad
sandwich she bought in the café. She had several cups of coffee as she worked through the afternoon
and had a muffin at 4 p.m. because she was beginning to get a headache. She met her friend Ciara for
a game of squash after work. On her way home she picked up a take-away and a soft drink for dinner.

    (a)  What are the problems with Rachel's diet?

    (b)  Suggest four ways she could improve it.

    (c)  Plan a healthy day's menu for Rachel.

2.  Make a selection of wall charts of the food pyramid and display them throughout the school.

3.  Calculate approximately how much time you spend on the following activities in a 24-hour period
    and present the information on a pie chart.

    ●  Sleeping
    ●  Eating
    ●  Studying, school work
    ●  Sport, walking, cycling
    ●  Relaxing, hobbies, watching TV

    Are there any changes you could make to improve your lifestyle?

4. Complete the crossword below.

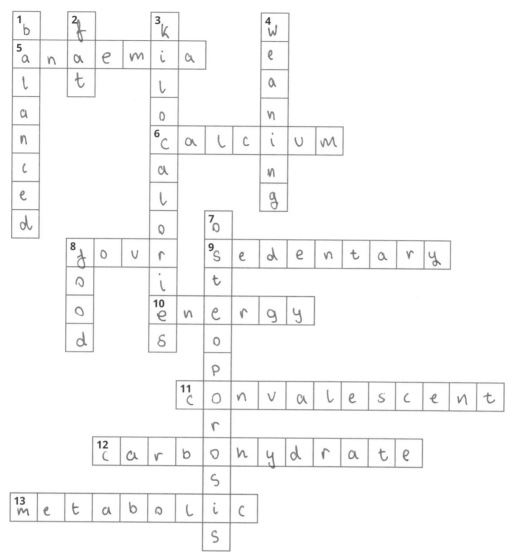

## Across

5. Iron helps to prevent ___anaemia___

6. Nutrient for healthy bones

8. The number of kilocalories in a gram of protein

9. Manual workers are more active than ___sedentary___ workers

10. ___energy___ is the ability to do work

11. A person recovering from illness

12. We should get most of our energy from this nutrient

13. The rate at which we use energy is our ___metabolic___ rate

## Down

1. A diet containing all the nutrients in the correct proportion

2. The nutrient that supplies the most energy

3. Units for measuring energy

4. Introducing babies to solid food

7. Bone disease of the elderly

8. What gives us our energy?

# Learning checklist

| Red: **I don't know this.** Orange: **I need to study this again.** Green: **Good to go!** | ● | ● | ● |
|---|:---:|:---:|:---:|
| I can define energy and energy balance. | ✓ | | |
| energy: the ability to do work    energy balance: matching energy intake with energy output | | | |
| I understand how energy is measured. | | ✓ | |
| I can differentiate between metabolic rate and basal metabolic rate. | ✓ | | |
| I can state the functions of energy. | | ✓ | |
| I can analyse the factors that affect energy requirements. | ✓ | | |
| I can define the term 'balanced diet'. | | | ✓ |
| I can explain the role of nutrients in contributing to a healthy balanced diet. | | | ✓ |
| I can identify the main food groups in the food pyramid and give examples of foods in each group. | ✓ | | |
| I can outline the healthy eating guidelines. | ✓ | | |
| I can plan balanced meals for people throughout the life cycle using the food pyramid and the healthy eating guidelines. | ✓ | | |
| I know the guidelines to follow when planning meals for pregnant women and convalescents. | ✓ | | |
| I can appreciate that nutritional needs differ at each stage of the life cycle. | ✓ | | |
| I can make informed decisions about nutrition and lifestyle in order to stay healthy. | ✓ | | |

**The topic I most enjoyed in this chapter:** _____

**The topic I would like to learn more about:** _____

# Special diets

## Obesity

1. (a) Explain what is meant by obesity. _____

_____

   (b) Suggest two reasons why people become overweight.

   (i) _____

   (ii) _____

2. Identify four health hazards linked with obesity.

   (a) _____

   (b) _____

   (c) _____

   (d) _____

3. Give two guidelines for achieving a healthy weight.

   (a) _____

   (b) _____

4. Name two eating disorders.

   (a) _____

   (b) _____

5. Recommend three lifestyle changes that could reduce the risk of developing obesity.

   (a) _____

   (b) _____

   (c) _____

## Vegetarians

1. Differentiate between vegan and lacto-vegetarian.

_____

_____

_____

2. Suggest reasons why someone might choose to become a vegetarian.

   (a) _____

   (b) _____

3. Explain what is meant by:

(a) Tofu _____

(b) TVP _____

(c) Quorn _____

4. Identify four foods that are unsuitable for a vegan.

(a) _____ (b) _____

(c) _____ (d) _____

5. Vegan diets require careful planning, as they may lack which four nutrients? Explain why.

_____

_____

6. Rewrite the menu, making adjustments to make it suitable for (a) a lacto-vegetarian and (b) a vegan.

| Egg mayonnaise<br>* * *<br>Chicken soup with white bread<br>* * *<br>Roast beef, carrots, parsnips<br>Roast potatoes<br>Gravy<br>* * *<br>Cheesecake and cream | Lacto-vegetarian menu | Vegan menu |
| --- | --- | --- |
| | | |

7. Explain why vegetarian diets are considered to be sustainable.

_____

_____

# Low-salt and low-cholesterol diets

1. State the RDA of:

(a) Salt _____ (b) Sodium _____

2. List three foods that are high in salt.

(a) _____ (b) _____ (c) _____

3. Suggest two ways of reducing salt in the diet.

(a) _____

(b) _____

4. (a) What is cholesterol? _____

   (b) Identify two possible side effects of cholesterol build-up.

   (i) _____

   (ii) _____

# Coeliac disease and diabetes

1. Outline the cause of coeliac disease.

   _____

   _____

2. List two symptoms of coeliac disease.

   (a) _____    (b) _____

3. List three foods that should be avoided by a person with coeliac disease.

   (a) _____    (b) _____    (c) _____

4. Draw the gluten-free symbol.

5. Design a two-course dinner menu suitable for a person with coeliac disease.

6. What is the cause of diabetes?

   _____

   _____

7. Distinguish between type 1 and type 2 diabetes.

| Type 1 diabetes | Type 2 diabetes |
| --- | --- |
|  |  |

8. The symptoms of diabetes are:

(a) _____

(b) _____

9. Outline two guidelines for the dietary treatment of diabetes.

(a) _____

(b) _____

10. Identify three foods that may cause an allergic reaction.

(a) _____

(b) _____

(c) _____

# High-fibre diet

1. Fibre is a _____ that cannot be _____ by the body but helps in the _____ of food.

2. Suggest two benefits of a high-fibre diet.

(a) _____

(b) _____

3. Explain what is meant by refined food.

_____

_____

4. Complete the following table.

| Refined food | Healthy alternative |
| --- | --- |
| White rice |  |
| White bread |  |
| Spaghetti |  |

5. Suggest ways in which you could easily increase the fibre content of your diet.

_____

_____

# Over to you 👆

1. Indicate whether the following statements are true or false.

| Statement | True | False |
|---|:---:|:---:|
| Anorexia nervosa is an eating disorder. | ○ | ○ |
| Lack of cholesterol causes diabetes. | ○ | ○ |
| Quorn is a meat alternative made from soya beans. | ○ | ○ |
| The recommended daily amount of salt is 10 g. | ○ | ○ |
| Type 1 diabetes can be treated by diet alone. | ○ | ○ |
| Refined foods are high in fibre. | ○ | ○ |
| Someone who is very overweight is said to be obese. | ○ | ○ |
| A lacto-vegetarian will eat dairy products. | ○ | ○ |
| Another name for salt is sodium chloride. | ○ | ○ |
| Vegans eat fish. | ○ | ○ |

2. Design a day's menu suitable for one of the following:

   **(a)** An overweight five-year-old

   **(b)** A lacto-vegetarian teenager

   **(c)** A pregnant woman

   **(d)** A diabetic man

   **(e)** An elderly person with high cholesterol

   **(f)** An adult with coeliac disease

| Breakfast | Lunch | Dinner |
|---|---|---|
|  |  |  |

3. Choose one of the dietary conditions in this chapter and carry out further research on the topic. Present your findings to the class.

# Learning checklist

| Red: I don't know this. Orange: I need to study this again. Green: Good to go! | ● | ● | ● |
|---|---|---|---|
| I can work with others to explore the management of diet-related diseases. | | | |
| I can explain what is meant by obesity and I know some reasons why people become obese. | | | |
| I can identify some problems associated with obesity and I can outline guidelines for the treatment of obesity. | | | |
| I can distinguish between vegans and lacto-vegetarians and I can plan meals suitable for both. | | | |
| I appreciate the dangers of too much salt in the diet and I know how to reduce salt intake. | | | |
| I know why high-cholesterol levels are bad for you and I know how to manage a low-cholesterol diet. | | | |
| I understand the cause, symptoms and treatment of coeliac disease. | | | |
| I can identify some foods that could cause an allergic reaction in the body. | | | |
| I can differentiate between type 1 and type 2 diabetes and I can outline the treatment for diabetes. | | | |
| I can give reasons why some people follow a high-fibre diet and I can outline how to plan high-fibre diets. | | | |
| I can apply my nutritional knowledge and be creative in planning meals for people with special dietary needs. | | | |

**The topic I most enjoyed in this chapter:** _____

**The topic I would like to learn more about:** _____

# Meal planning 5

1. Arrange the points on eating well throughout the day on p. 52 of your textbook in order of importance to you.

_____

_____

_____

_____

_____

_____

2. Outline four considerations when planning meals.

(a) _____

(b) _____

(c) _____

(d) _____

# Breakfasts

1. Explain why it is important for teenagers to eat a nourishing breakfast.

_____

_____

_____

_____

2. Fill in the following table, showing the main nutrients of each food in this breakfast. State the function of each nutrient.

| Food | Nutrient | Function |
|---|---|---|
| Apple segments | | |
| Porridge | | |
| Milk | | |
| Wholegrain bread | | |
| Butter | | |
| Marmalade | | |

# Packed meals

1. Outline two points to consider when planning packed meals.

    (a) _____

    (b) _____

2. Match the foods with a suitable type of packaging:

| Food | Packaging |
|------|-----------|
| Ham sandwiches | Tinfoil |
| Yoghurt | Lunchbox |
| Apple | Thermos flask |
| Chicken leg | Plastic bottle |
| Tomato soup | Plastic carton |
| Sausage roll | Greaseproof paper |
| Orange juice | Plastic bag |

3. Design a balanced packed lunch suitable for (a) a sedentary worker and (b) an active school-going teenager.

| Sedentary worker | School-going teenager |
|------------------|----------------------|
|                  |                      |

# Starters and soups

1. What is the purpose of a starter in a meal?

    _____

    _____

    _____

**2.** Give one example of a starter using each of the following foods:

| Food | Starter |
|------|---------|
| Fruit | |
| Vegetable | |
| Fish | |
| Meat | |

**3.** Complete the following sentences:

(a) Stock is a liquid in which _____ or _____ bones and vegetables have

been _____ gently for a long time.

(b) Stock is used in _____ and sauces

to improve _____

and _____.

**4.** Examine the labelling on the stock and complete the following:

(a) What flavour is the stock? _____

(b) List the six main ingredients

_____   _____

_____   _____

_____   _____

(c) How much sodium is present in the stock?

_____

(d) What is the danger of a diet high in salt?

_____

**Chicken stock**

**Ingredients**
Salt, potato starch, vegetable fat, yeast extract, sugar, chicken fat (2%), chicken powder (1%), spices (turmeric, white pepper and celery seeds), flavourings, onion, parsley, colour (caramel), antioxidant

**Nutritive value per 100ml stock**
Protein 0.1g
Carbohydrate 2.6g
Fat 0.5g
Sodium 0.36g

**5.** Suggest reasons for the following guidelines for making soup:

| Rule | Reason |
|------|--------|
| Use a heavy saucepan with a tight-fitting lid. | |
| Sauté vegetables. | |
| Blend thickeners. | |
| Use homemade stock. | |

6. The following label is from a packet of convenience soup.

Using the information given right, answer each of the following.

**Country Garden Soup**

**Cooking instructions**
1. Add 850 ml cold water.
2. Bring to boil, stirring occasionally.
3. Cover and simmer for 5 minutes.
4. Garnish and serve.

| Nutritional information per 250 ml serving | Ingredients |
|---|---|
| Energy 98 kcal | Tomato powder, |
| Protein 1.8 g | Sugar, Wheat |
| Carbohydrate 14.5 g | flour, Modified |
| Fat 1.5 g | starch, Salt, |
| Sodium 1.0 g | Vegetable oils, |
| Fibre 0.5 g | Flavourings |

(a) Name the main ingredient in the soup.

(b) How long should the soup be simmered for?

(c) Name three nutrients found in the soup.

(i) _____

(ii) _____

(iii) _____

(d) How much fibre is provided per 250 ml serving of the soup?

(e) Suggest one way of improving the fibre content of the soup.

7. Design three-course dinner menus for (a) a special occasion and (b) an economical meal.

8. If 1 kg of flour costs €2.20 calculate the cost of the following amounts:

| Amount | Cost |
|---|---|
| 200 g | |
| 500 g | |
| 100 g | |

# Over to you ☞

1. (a) Design one day's menus (breakfast, lunch and dinner) suitable for family weekend meals.

(b) Cost the main course dinner dish.

| | Cost |
|---|---|
| _____ | |
| _____ | |
| _____ | |

2. **(a)** Soup can be processed in many different ways. It is available canned, dried 'instant' (as in 'cup-a-soup') and chilled in cartons. Homemade soup is easy to make. Working in groups, prepare a homemade soup. Prepare and serve a number of samples of the same flavour of convenience soups. Set up a taste panel. Compare the homemade soups with the convenience soups. Record your findings as follows.

| Types of soup | Preparation and cooking time | Cost per portion | Convenience of preparation | Preference |
|---|---|---|---|---|
| | | | | |
| | | | | |
| | | | | |
| | | | | |

**(b)** Compare the ingredients used in each type of soup. Which ingredients did they all have in common?

**(c)** What ingredients were in (i) the canned soup and (ii) the dried soup that were not in the homemade soup?

**(d)** Research the function of three additives used in commercial soups.

3. Find these words about meal planning in the word search below.

APPETISER     DIPS     NUTRITION     SMOOTHIES
BREAKFAST     FRUIT     NUTS     STARTER
CRUDITÉS     LUNCH     OCCASION     STOCK
DESSERT     MENU     SALAD     VARIETY

| F | R | I | S | K | Y | H | W | N | X | L | G | A | T | K |
|---|---|---|---|---|---|---|---|---|---|---|---|---|---|---|
| Y | E | Z | X | M | Z | C | O | U | N | E | M | B | Q | A |
| S | T | O | D | E | O | I | S | É | T | I | D | U | R | C |
| P | R | E | N | D | T | O | T | K | P | R | P | A | O | T |
| I | A | O | I | I | X | R | T | U | Y | Z | C | P | B | V |
| D | T | I | R | R | E | J | W | H | X | S | M | P | X | X |
| P | S | T | L | S | A | F | N | K | I | K | M | E | F | M |
| K | U | T | S | Q | X | V | B | M | P | E | O | T | R | O |
| N | J | E | S | L | U | N | C | H | Y | C | S | I | U | P |
| Y | D | O | O | A | D | B | E | S | C | F | S | S | I | Y |
| T | D | J | M | H | L | H | Y | A | T | T | G | E | T | B |
| B | R | E | A | K | F | A | S | T | O | U | Z | R | Y | Z |
| P | F | Y | I | X | Q | I | D | C | D | P | N | U | D | F |
| V | X | N | D | F | O | O | K | K | H | P | A | L | Y | H |
| C | X | V | G | N | V | E | Z | H | O | U | Z | T | C | U |

# Learning checklist

**Red: I don't know this. Orange: I need to study this again. Green: Good to go!**  ● ● ●

| | | | |
|---|---|---|---|
| I appreciate the importance of eating well throughout the day. | | | |
| I can apply the factors to consider when planning nutritious meals. | | | |
| I can evaluate meals and snacks in terms of nutritive value. | | | |
| I understand the importance of a healthy breakfast. | | | |
| I can outline the factors to consider when planning packed lunches. | | | |
| I can identify some healthy snacks. | | | |
| I know why a starter may be served and I know suitable foods for starters. | | | |
| I know what stock is and what it is used for. | | | |
| I can apply some guidelines for making soup. | | | |
| I know some suitable garnishes and accompaniments for soups. | | | |
| I can plan, cost and evaluate menus for breakfast, lunch and dinner. | | | |
| I can use apps and websites to assist in the planning of healthy balanced meals. | | | |

**The topic I most enjoyed in this chapter:** _____

**The topic I would like to learn more about:** _____

# Food safety and hygiene

1. Explain the role of each of the following in food spoilage:

   (a) Enzymes _____

   _____

   (b) Microorganisms _____

   _____

2. State three conditions that favour the growth of bacteria.

   (a) _____

   (b) _____

   (c) _____

3. Match the temperature in column A with the effect of the temperature on bacteria in column B.

| A: Temperature range | B: Effect on bacteria |
| --- | --- |
| 1–4°C | Most bacteria are killed |
| 30–40°C | Slow down growth |
| –18 to –25°C | Bacteria grow and multiply |
| 100°C | Inactivate bacteria |

4. What does the term 'danger zone' mean?

   _____

   _____

5. Shade in the danger zone on the diagram.

100°C
95°C
90°C
85°C
80°C
75°C
70°C
65°C
60°C
55°C
50°C
45°C
40°C
35°C
30°C
25°C
20°C
15°C
10°C
5°C
0°C
-5°C
-10°C
-15°C
-20°C
-25°C

6. (a) Bacteria carriers transfer _____ on to _____.

   (b) Give three examples of bacteria carriers.

       (i) _____   (ii) _____   (iii) _____

7. Identify two types of bacteria that cause food poisoning.

   (a) _____   (b) _____

8. Which type of bacteria is the most commonly reported cause of food poisoning in Ireland?

   _____

9. Four symptoms of food poisoning are:

   (a) _____   (b) _____

   (c) _____   (d) _____

10. Explain the following terms.

   (a) Shelf life: _____

   (b) Perishable: _____

11. Suggest two advantages of storing food correctly.

   (a) _____

   (b) _____

12. (a) Explain why wall units are recommended for food storage.

   _____

   _____

   (b) Why should raw meat be stored below cooked meat in the fridge?

   _____

   _____

13. Indicate on the diagram where each of the following foods should be stored:

   a Raw meat
   b Lettuce
   c Eggs
   d Bread
   e Onions
   f Potatoes
   g Milk
   h Apples
   i Flour
   j Tinned tomatoes

**14.** Suggest one reason in each case for the following food storage rules.

(a) Use food in rotation: _____

(b) Keep perishable food refrigerated: _____

(c) Check expiry dates: _____

**15.** Give two rules under each heading: Food hygiene and Kitchen hygiene.

(a) _____

(b) _____

**16.** Explain what is meant by cross-contamination. _____

_____

**17.** Examine the case study and answer the questions that follow.

# Case study

It was a lovely day so Jason and his friends decided to go on a trek. They raided the fridge and filled a rucksack with food. They hiked for many hours in the warm sunshine, then set up camp. The fire was slow to start and did not give off much heat – just enough to cook the sausages. During the night, the boys developed nausea, abdominal pain and vomiting.

(a) What is the likely source of the food-poisoning bacteria?

_____

_____

_____

(b) Suggest some bacteria that could be a possible cause of this food poisoning.

_____

_____

_____

(c) Suggest some precautions Jason could have taken to make food poisoning less likely to have occurred.

_____

_____

_____

_____

_____

_____

_____

_____

_____

**18.** Circle the possible causes of food poisoning in the picture shown below.

# Safety in the kitchen

**1.** Suggest two rules for electrical safety in the kitchen.

(a) _____

(b) _____

**2.** State one safety rule for each of the following:

|  | Safety rule |
|---|---|
| Preparing food |  |
| Cooking food |  |

**3.** Most accidents that occur in the home happen in the kitchen. Suggest one reason why this is so.

_____

**4.** Mark six possible causes of accidents in the picture shown below.

# Over to you 👆

1. Discuss and identify a reason for each of the following rules.

| Rule | Reasons |
| --- | --- |
| Use separate surfaces when preparing raw and cooked foods. | |
| Do not prepare food for others if you are sick. | |
| Keep kitchen clean and well ventilated. | |
| Keep the kitchen bin covered and empty it regularly. | |
| Put perishable food in the fridge as soon as possible after buying. | |
| Reheat leftovers thoroughly before eating them. | |

2. Design and create posters to encourage hygiene and safety in food storage, handling, preparation and cooking, and display them in the Home Economics room.

# Learning checklist

| Red: **I don't know this.** Orange: **I need to study this again.** Green: **Good to go!** | 🔴 | ⚫ | ⚪ |
| --- | --- | --- | --- |
| I can state two causes of food spoilage. | | | |
| I can name three types of microorganisms that cause food spoilage. | | | |
| I can describe four conditions for the growth of microorganisms. | | | |
| I can explain what the danger zone means. | | | |
| I can identify some bacteria carriers. | | | |
| I can explain what causes food poisoning and list the symptoms. | | | |
| I have basic knowledge of some common food-poisoning bacteria. | | | |
| I can apply some rules for safe food storage. | | | |
| I can apply some rules for food handling, and food and kitchen hygiene in order to avoid food poisoning. | | | |

**The topic I most enjoyed in this chapter:** _____

**The topic I would like to learn more about:** _____

# 7 Food preparation

**1. (a)** What is a recipe?

_____

**(b)** Suggest two reasons why a recipe should be followed accurately.

**(i)** _____

**(ii)** _____

**2.** Rewrite the following instructions for baking in the correct order.

| | | |
|---|---|---|
| Weigh ingredient | **1.** | _____ |
| Collect equipment | **2.** | _____ |
| Prepare tins | **3.** | _____ |
| Read recipe | **4.** | _____ |
| Put on apron | **5.** | _____ |
| Wash hands | **6.** | _____ |

**3.** Complete the following table.

| Spoons | Ml |
|---|---|
| 1 teaspoon | |
| | 15 ml |
| 1 dessertspoon | |

**4.** Match the pieces of equipment in the picture with the list below.

**(a)** Palate knife _____  **(b)** Perforated spoon _____  **(c)** Vegetable peeler _____

**(d)** Sieve _____  **(e)** Spatula _____  **(f)** Grater _____

**(g)** Fish slice _____  **(h)** Soup ladle _____  **(i)** Weighing scales _____

**(j)** Whisk _____  **(k)** Vegetable masher _____  **(l)** Measuring jug _____

**5.** Fill in the temperatures below.

(a) Boiling point = _____ °C    (b) Freezing point = _____ °C

(c) Moderate oven = _____ °C  (d) Hot oven = _____ °C

**6.** (a) What is meant by preheating an oven? _____

(b) How would you know if an electric oven is fully preheated?

_____

**7.** State one rule each for the use, care, safety and energy-efficiency when using food-preparation appliances.

| Use | Care | Safety | Energy efficiency |
|-----|------|--------|-------------------|
|     |      |        |                   |
|     |      |        |                   |
|     |      |        |                   |

**8.** Suggest a reason for each of the following rules.

| Rule | Reasons |
|------|---------|
| Do not run a food-preparation appliance for a long period. | |
| Unplug food-preparation appliances when cleaning. | |

**9.** State three uses in each case of the following:

(a) Food mixers

(i) _____    (ii) _____    (iii) _____

(b) Blenders/liquidisers

(i) _____    (ii) _____    (iii) _____

(c) Food processors

(i) _____    (ii) _____    (iii) _____

**10.** Describe how to clean a food mixer.

_____

_____

_____

_____

_____

_____

# Over to you ☝

1. Find the following words in the word search about food preparation.

| | | | |
|---|---|---|---|
| APRON | EQUIPMENT | METHOD | SCALES |
| BRINE | GARNISH | MILLILITRES | SIEVE |
| CENTIGRADE | INGREDIENTS | MIXER | SIMMER |
| CROUTONS | KILOGRAMS | MODERATE | SOLIDS |
| CUTLERY | LIQUIDISER | RECIPE | TABLESPOON |
| DOUGH | LIQUIDS | RESOURCES | WEIGH |
| DOILY | MEASURE | | |

| | | | | | | | | | | | | | |
|---|---|---|---|---|---|---|---|---|---|---|---|---|---|
| C | U | T | L | E | R | Y | K | E | P | I | C | E | R | S |
| D | O | I | L | Y | E | Q | I | H | G | I | E | W | K | N |
| G | S | S | I | E | V | E | L | C | N | L | N | N | O | O |
| U | H | S | E | C | R | U | O | S | E | R | O | N | H | T |
| L | Z | S | S | D | O | U | G | H | A | T | O | S | R | U |
| S | T | N | E | I | D | E | R | G | N | I | P | E | L | O |
| E | U | E | I | R | R | K | A | Z | B | M | S | L | I | R |
| A | T | E | Q | U | T | R | M | K | Y | I | E | A | Q | C |
| D | A | A | S | U | N | I | S | D | D | X | L | C | U | S |
| T | O | A | R | I | I | I | L | I | J | E | B | S | I | O |
| S | E | H | S | E | M | P | U | I | N | R | A | U | D | L |
| M | X | H | T | M | D | Q | M | I | L | O | T | T | S | I |
| I | Z | R | E | E | I | O | R | E | R | L | R | Z | V | D |
| A | I | R | A | L | M | B | M | X | N | M | I | P | I | S |
| C | E | N | T | I | G | R | A | D | E | T | L | M | A | T |

2. (a) Look up the recipe for apple and blueberry crumble on p. 175 of your textbook. Read the recipe and make out the equipment list needed to make this dish.

   (b) Draw the set-up of your unit to make the apple and blueberry crumble.

3. (a) Visit a local electrical shop or research online and make a list of six different kitchen appliances for sale.

(b) Complete the following table on the six appliances.

| Appliance | Brand name | Cost | Uses |
|---|---|---|---|
| | | | |
| | | | |
| | | | |
| | | | |
| | | | |
| | | | |

# Learning checklist

**Red: I don't know this.** Orange: **I need to study this again.** Green: **Good to go!** ● ● ●

I can explain what a recipe is and how to follow one.

I can apply the order of work to follow when preparing for a practical class.

I understand how to make a list of equipment and how to organise the table set-up.

I can explain how to weigh and measure ingredients.

I can demonstrate my culinary skills in the preparation for practical classes.

I have researched some technology available for food preparation.

I understand how to safely use and care for electrical appliances.

**The topic I most enjoyed in this chapter:** _____

**The topic I would like to learn more about:** _____

# 8 Cooking food

1. Fill in the missing words. Food is cooked:

   To kill _____ making food _____ _____ _____.

   To improve _____ making food taste nicer.

   To improve _____ making food look appetising.

2. Nutrients change during cooking. Fill in the missing words to complete the following paragraph:

   Protein _____ and _____. Fat _____.

   Water _____. Some _____ and _____

   are lost. _____ _____ swell, burst and absorb liquid.

3. Suggest two disadvantages of overcooking food.

   (a) _____

   (b) _____

4. Define the three methods of heat transfer.

   | Conduction |
   | Convection |
   | Radiation |

5. (a) State two examples of each of the following cooking methods.

   | Moist methods | Dry methods | Methods using fat |
   |---|---|---|
   |  |  |  |
   |  |  |  |

   (b) List two examples of suitable foods and state one advantage in each case.

   | Moist methods | Suitable foods | Advantage |
   |---|---|---|
   | Boiling |  |  |
   | Poaching |  |  |
   | Steaming |  |  |
   | Pressure cooking |  |  |

6. Explain why stewing is a better method of cooking than boiling.

   _____

   _____

7. Draw a labelled diagram of a pressure cooker. Name two foods that could be cooked by this method.

(a) _____

(b) _____

8. (a) Baking is cooking food by _____ _____ in an oven by _____.

   (b) Grilling is cooking food by _____ _____ at a high _____.

9. Complete the following table:

| Dry method | Suitable foods | Guidelines |
|---|---|---|
| Roasting | | |
| Grilling | | |

10. Explain how a meat thermometer can be used when roasting meat.

_____

_____

_____

_____

**11.** What are the advantages of grilling rather than frying food?

_____

_____

_____

_____

**12.** Suggest two disadvantages of grilling.

(a) _____

(b) _____

**13.** Distinguish between shallow-fat frying and deep-fat frying.

_____

_____

_____

_____

**14.** Complete the table for cooking methods using fat.

| Food | Suitable coating | Reason for coating |
| --- | --- | --- |
|  |  |  |
|  |  |  |

# Microwave cooking

**1.** Complete the following paragraph.

A microwave oven produces _____ _____, which are directed into

the _____. These waves cause the _____ within the _____

to _____ rapidly. This friction causes _____, so that the food cooks

from within by _____.

**2.** Microwave ovens have many uses. Complete the table below.

| Use | Example |
| --- | --- |
|  |  |
|  |  |
|  |  |

**3.** Explain how microwave rating or wattage affects cooking time.

_____

_____

_____

**4.** Suggest a reason for each of the following guidelines for using microwave ovens.

| Guideline | Reason |
|---|---|
| Pierce the skin of potatoes before microwaving. | |
| Allow soup to stand for a few minutes after reheating it in a microwave oven. | |
| Do not use very light plastic food containers in a microwave oven. | |

**5.** State two guidelines to follow in each case.

| Caring for a microwave oven | Cleaning a microwave oven |
|---|---|
| | |
| | |

**6.** Outline the function of the turntable in a microwave oven.

_____

_____

_____

**7.** Suggest four ways to save money and energy when cooking food.

(a) _____

_____

_____

(b) _____

_____

_____

(c) _____

_____

_____

(d) _____

_____

_____

# Over to you 👉

1. Complete the crossword on cooking methods.

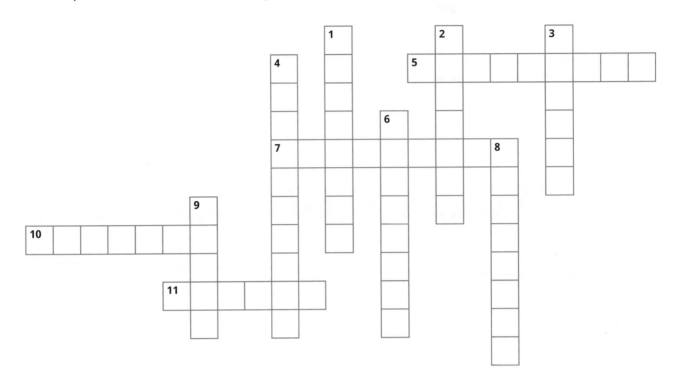

## Across

5. Method of heat transfer used in grilling

7. Common use of a microwave oven

10. The ____ of a microwave determines the cooking time

11. Dry method of cooking in an oven

## Down

1. Gentle method of cooking for delicate foods

2. Spooning hot fat over roasting meat

3. ____ grains swell and burst when heated

4. Method of cooking often carried out in a wok

6. ____ are destroyed when food is cooked

8. Method of cooking that reduces fat

9. No ____ utensils should be used in a microwave oven

2. Frying is the most dangerous method of cooking. Design a slogan that could be displayed in the Home Economics room to warn people to be careful when frying food.

3. Consult the table below and answer the questions that follow.

| Roasting | | |
|---|---|---|
| Meat | Temperature | Time |
| Beef (medium) | 180°C/gas 4 | 25 minutes per 500 g plus 25 minutes |
| Lamb (well done) | 180°C/gas 4 | 30 minutes per 500 g plus 30 minutes |
| Pork (well done) | 180°C/gas 4 | 35 minutes per 500 g plus 30 minutes |
| Chicken | 200°C/gas 6 | 20 minutes per 500 g plus 20 minutes |

(a)  Which meat takes longest to cook per 500 g? _____

Which meat takes the least amount of time to cook per 500 g?_____

(b)  1 kg = 1,000 g. Calculate how long it would take to roast:

   (i)  3 kg leg of lamb _____   (ii) 1 kg chicken _____

(c)  What is a meat thermometer? _____

(d)  What should the internal temperature of meat be when cooked? _____

(e)  Why is it important that this temperature is reached? _____

# Learning checklist

| Red: I don't know this. Orange: I need to study this again. Green: Good to go! | ● | ● | ● |
|---|---|---|---|
| I appreciate why food is cooked and the changes that occur when food is cooked. | | | |
| I understand the three methods of heat transfer. | | | |
| I am able to classify the cooking methods. | | | |
| I can think critically about the advantages and disadvantages of each method of cooking. | | | |
| I know a definition, suitable foods and guidelines for each method of cooking. | | | |
| I understand why food is coated before cooking. | | | |
| I can apply a range of cooking principles and techniques in the preparation of healthy meals and snacks. | | | |
| I have researched some appliances that are used in food planning and preparation. | | | |
| I can apply budgetary considerations when cooking family meals. | | | |

**The topic I most enjoyed in this chapter:** _____

**The topic I would like to learn more about:** _____

# 9 Meat, fish and protein alternatives

## Meat

1. Give the source of each of the following meats.

| Bacon | Veal | Beef | Venison | Pork | Mutton |
|-------|------|------|---------|------|--------|
|       |      |      |         |      |        |

2. State one function of each of the following nutrients found in meat:

   (a) Protein _____

   (b) Vitamin B _____

   (c) Iron _____

3. (a) Meat lacks carbohydrate and Vitamin C. Give one function for each of these nutrients .

| Nutrient | Function |
|----------|----------|
| Carbohydrate | |
| Vitamin C | |

   (b) Apply your knowledge of nutrition and design a three-course dinner menu that includes meat and incorporates these two nutrients.

4. Draw a labelled diagram of the structure of meat.

5. Suggest four causes of toughness in meat.

   (a) _____    (b) _____

   (c) _____    (d) _____

6. Outline two methods of tenderising meat.

   (a) _____

   (b) _____

7. (a) State three dishes that can be made using minced meat.

   (i) _____  (ii) _____  (iii) _____

   (b) Suggest one point to follow when buying, storing and cooking minced meat.

| Buying minced meat | Storing minced meat | Cooking minced meat |
|---|---|---|
|  |  |  |

8. The following is a list of ingredients for homemade beef burgers:

   400 g minced beef                 15 g breadcrumbs

   25 g diced onion seasoning      1 egg

   (a) Use the information given above and answer any of the following:

   (i) What is the main ingredient in the recipe?

   _____

   (ii) What ingredient is used to bind burgers?

   _____

   (iii) Suggest a seasoning for the burgers.

   _____

   (iv) Name another ingredient that could be added to improve the flavour of the burgers.

   _____

**(b)** Plan a two-course menu for a teenager that includes a homemade burger.

9. Examine the cuts of beef below and answer the following questions. Remember tough cuts of meat require moist slow cooking.

# Cuts of beef

1. **Neck/chuck/shoulder:** Stewing and minced meat dishes

2. **Rib:** Stewing, braising, roasting

3. **Top rib/housekeeper's cut:** Braising

4. **Shin:** Stock making

5. **Brisket (boned and rolled):** Boiling (corned or spiced)

6. **Rib:** Stewing, braising, roasting

7. **Rolled rib:** Roasting

8. **Fillet:** Frying, grilling
   ● **Sirloin:** Frying
   ● **Striploin:** Frying, grilling

9. **Flank:** Stewing (minced meat dishes)

10. **Eye of the round:** Stewing (minced meat)
    ● **Silverside (part of round):** Boiled (corned), braising
    ● **Topside (part of round):** Stewing, braising

11. **Ball of the round:** Stewing, braising

12. **Hind, shin:** Stock making

**(a)** Identify three tough cuts of meat. How might these cuts be tenderised in the home before cooking?

(i) _____    (ii) _____    (iii) _____

_____

**(b)** Name three tender cuts of beef. How do you know that these are tender cuts?

(i) _____    (ii) _____    (iii) _____

_____

**(c)** Why do you think that some cuts are only suitable for making stock?

_____

**(d)** Suggest some information you would expect to find on prepackaged meat.

(i) _____    (ii) _____

(iii) _____    (iv) _____

**10.** What information does this symbol convey to the consumer?

_____

_____

BORD BIA
QUALITY
ASSURANCE SCHEME
ORIGIN-IRELAND

**11.** Fill in two points on each of the following headings:

| Reasons for cooking meat | Effects of cooking on meat |
|---|---|
|  |  |
|  |  |

**12.** Match the meat in column A with a suitable accompanying sauce in column B.

| A | B |
|---|---|
| Roast beef | Apple sauce |
| Roast chicken | Orange sauce |
| Roast pork | Horseradish sauce |
| Roast duck | Mint sauce |
| Roast lamb | Cranberry sauce |

**13.** Give one reason for each of the following:

**(a)** Eating red meat is good for a teenager with anaemia.

_____

_____

**(b)** Mincing tenderises meat.

_____

_____

**(c)** Store raw meat below cooked meat in the fridge.

_____

_____

**(d)** Meat shrinks when cooked.

_____

_____

**14.** Suggest one guideline for each of the following:

**(a)** Buying fresh chicken _____

**(b)** Buying frozen chicken _____

**(c)** Storing fresh chicken _____

**(d)** Storing frozen chicken _____

**15.** Explain why is essential to cook poultry thoroughly.

_____

_____

**16. (a)** What is offal? _____

**(b)** State three examples of offal.

**(i)** _____  **(ii)** _____  **(iii)** _____

**(c)** Suggest one advantage and one disadvantage of including offal in the diet.

| Advantage | Disadvantage |
|---|---|
|  |  |

**(d)** List two dishes that include offal.

**(i)** _____

**(ii)** _____

**17.** List four meat products.

**(a)** _____

**(b)** _____

**(c)** _____

**(d)** _____

# Protein alternatives

**1.** Complete the following sentences on protein alternatives:

**(a)** TVP is made from _____ _____. It is available _____ ,

in chunks or in products such as _____. It is cheaper to produce

than _____.

**(b)** Quorn is a _____ _____ developed from _____

e.g. _____. It is low in _____ and high in _____

and _____.

**2.** Examine the information on the label.

**(a)** What is the main nutrient found in Quorn pieces?

_____

**(b)** What are the three main ingredients in the product?

**(i)** _____  **(ii)** _____  **(iii)** _____

**(c)** How is it stored in the home? _____

**(d)** How long does it take to cook? _____

**(e)** How many grams in a recommended portion? How many grams of Quorn should be used if the meal was for four people? _____

_____

**(f)** What symbol on the label indicates that the product is not very damaging to the environment?

_____

# Fish

**1.** Research some recipes for suitable fish dishes in each case.

| Use | Example |
| --- | --- |
| Breakfast | |
| Starter | |
| Main course | |
| Packed lunch | |

2. Name the vitamins found in fish and investigate one function of each.

| Vitamin | Function |
| --- | --- |
|  |  |
|  |  |
|  |  |

3. Name the minerals found in fish and investigate one function of each.

| Mineral | Function |
| --- | --- |
|  |  |
|  |  |

4. Suggest two advantages of including fish rather than meat in the diet.

(a) _____  (b) _____

5. Outline two points to follow when buying fresh fish.

(a) _____

(b) _____

6. Explain the term 'in season' in relation to fish.

_____

7. State two advantages of buying fish when in season.

(a) _____  (b) _____

8. Fill in the following table on the storage of fish.

| Storing fresh fish | Storing frozen fish |
| --- | --- |
|  |  |
|  |  |
|  |  |

9. List three methods of preserving fish giving two examples in each case.

(a) _____

(b) _____

(c) _____

10. Explain what is meant by the term 'brine' and state the effect it has on the nutritive value of a food.

_____

_____

_____

11. Research online or using books find some recipes and complete the following table.

| Methods of cooking fish | Suitable fish |
|---|---|
| Frying | |
| Grilling/barbecuing | |
| Poaching | |

12. Set out a three-course dinner menu using fish in the main course. Suggest a suitable garnish and sauce.

13. Suggest two ways of encouraging children to eat fish.

(a) _____

(b) _____

# Over to you

1. Research some recipes using each of the following foods. Fill in the dishes in the table below.

| Minced beef | Fish | Chicken | Offal | Protein alternatives |
|---|---|---|---|---|
| | | | | |

2. Visit a local supermarket and investigate the following:

(a) The range of chilled and frozen chicken products available.

(b) The range of meat alternatives such as TVP, tofu and Quorn available tinned, frozen or chilled.

(c) Find out the cost of tinned salmon. How does it compare with the cost of fresh salmon? (Remember to consider the weight.)

# Learning checklist

**Red: I don't know this. Orange: I need to study this again. Green: Good to go!**  ● ● ●

| | | | |
|---|---|---|---|
| I can outline the nutritive value of meat and appreciate its value in the diet. | | | |
| I can draw and label a diagram of the structure of meat. | | | |
| I understand what causes toughness and ways of tenderising meat. | | | |
| I can explain how to buy, store and cook meat and poultry safely. | | | |
| I can state the effects of cooking on meat. | | | |
| I can outline the nutritive value of poultry. | | | |
| I can explain what is meant by offal and meat products and can give examples of each. | | | |
| I can explore options and alternative sources of protein and outline the advantages of including them in the diet. | | | |
| I can classify fish and I understand the nutritional value and the value of fish in the diet. | | | |
| I can apply my knowledge when buying fish and storing fish. | | | |
| I can suggest methods for preserving fish and give examples. | | | |
| I understand how cooking affects fish. | | | |
| I can recommend suitable coatings, sauces and garnishes for fish. | | | |
| I can express my opinion when evaluating and comparing meat, fish and protein alternatives and their products. | | | |

**The topic I most enjoyed in this chapter:** _____

**The topic I would like to learn more about:** _____

# Milk, cheese and eggs

**10**

## Milk

**1. (a)** Milk is regarded as a 'complete food'. Explain this statement.

_____

_____

**(b)** Indicate one animal source and one plant source of milk.

**(i)** _____  **(ii)** _____

**(c)** This plant source of milk is particularly important in the diet of _____.

**2.** State one mineral and one vitamin lacking in milk and give two sources of each.

|         |  | Source | Source |
|---------|--|--------|--------|
| Mineral |  |        |        |
| Vitamin |  |        |        |

**3.** Indicate whether each of the following is true or false.

| Statement | True | False |
|-----------|------|-------|
| Milk is made up of mainly of water. | ○ | ○ |
| Milk is an important source of vitamin C. | ○ | ○ |
| Milk sugar is called sucrose. | ○ | ○ |
| Low fat milk has more calories than whole milk. | ○ | ○ |
| Calcium is for healthy bones and teeth. | ○ | ○ |
| Protein is reduced in skimmed milk. | ○ | ○ |

**4.** As milk is an easily digested food it is particularly important in the diets of:

**(a)** _____

**(b)** _____

**(c)** _____

**5.** State the nutrient in milk responsible for the following:

| Function | Nutrient |
|---|---|
| Growth | |
| Release of energy from food | |
| Healthy teeth | |

**6.** Explain why it is important to store milk correctly.

_____

**7.** List two methods of processing milk.

(a) _____

(b) _____

**8.** Complete the following table for pasteurisation:

| Process involved | Effect |
|---|---|
| | |
| | |
| | |

**9.** Research four different types of milk available in supermarkets. Suggest one use for each.

| Type | Use |
|---|---|
| | |
| | |
| | |
| | |

**10.** Suggest two examples of the uses of milk in each case:

| Uses of milk | Examples |
|---|---|
| In baking | |
| As a drink | |
| In sauces | |
| In savoury dishes | |
| In desserts | |
| In soups | |
| In sauces | |
| In milk puddings | |

# Milk products

1. Name four dairy products that are available in supermarkets.

   (a) _____  (b) _____

   (c) _____  (d) _____

2. The following information is displayed on the label of a fruit smoothie drink.

   | Nutritional information | | | |
   |---|---|---|---|
   | | Typical value per 100 ml | GDA for a typical adult | Ingredients |
   | Energy | 56 kcal | 2,000 kcal | Pasteurised whole milk, apples, raspberries, strawberries, blueberries |
   | Protein | 0.4 g | | |
   | Carbohydrate | 14.0 g | 90 g | |
   | Fat | 3.0 g | 70 g | |
   | Fibre | 0.6 g | 35 g | |
   | Vitamin C | 40.0 mg | | |

   (a) Evaluate the nutritional value of the fruit smoothie drink.

   _____

   _____

   _____

   (b) What is meant by the term 'whole milk'?

   _____

   _____

   (c) Why is milk pasteurised? Explain how this procedure is carried out.

   _____

   _____

   _____

3. (a) Butter is particularly high in which nutrient? _____

   (b) Suggest one advantage of including bio-yoghurts in the diet.

   _____

4. Suggest three uses of yoghurt in the diet.

   (a) _____

   (b) _____

   (c) _____

5.  Examine the information on the yoghurt label and complete the following:

    (a)  List the three main ingredients in this yoghurt.

        (i)  _____

        (ii)  _____

        (iii)  _____

    (b)  How much sugar is in the yoghurt? _____

    (c)  Name two additives in the yoghurt.

        (i)  _____

        (ii)  _____

    (d)  State four pieces of information found on the label.

        (i)  _____

        (ii)  _____

        (iii)  _____

        (iv)  _____

**Low-fat organic strawberry yoghurt**

Ingredients
Organic low-fat milk, organic skimmed milk powder, organic strawberries (8%), sugar, lemon juice, stabiliser, flavouring, active cultures

Nutritive value per 100g
Protein 4.8g
Fat 1.6g
Carbohydrate 13.1g
  of which are sugars 12.8g

| 450g | Best before – use by 9/9/19 |
|---|---|

Store between 0–4°C

# Cheese

1.  Complete the following sentences about making cheese.

    (a)  A culture of _____ is added to _____. The milk is _____slightly.

    (b)  _____ is added to separate the milk into _____ and _____.

    (c)  The curds are drained, _____ and _____. The_____is removed.

    (d)  The cheese is pressed into _____ and left to _____.

2.  Insert each cheese into the correct classification in the table below: Cheddar, Edam, Brie, cheese spreads, cottage, Parmesan, foil wrapped cheese, Gouda.

| Hard | Soft | Semi hard | Processed |
|---|---|---|---|
|  |  |  |  |
|  |  |  |  |

3.  Cheddar cheese is mainly composed of which three nutrients (include the percentage)?

    (a)  _____        (b)  _____        (c)  _____

4.  Complete the following sentences:

    (a)  The mineral c _____and s _____ are found in cheese.

    (b)  Vitamins _____, _____ and _____ are found in cheese.

**5.** Suggest two carbohydrate foods that could be eaten with cheese.

(a) _____ (b) _____

# The uses of cheese

**6.** Complete the following table on the uses of cheese.

| (a) | (b) |
|---|---|
| (c) | (d) |

**7.** Design and set out a two-course menu, to include cheese as the main ingredient, suitable for a family meal.

**8.** Suggest two ways of making cheese more digestible.

(a) _____ (b) _____

**9. (a)** How many daily servings of dairy are recommended in the food pyramid? _____

(b) Suggest four ways you could increase dairy consumption.

(i) _____ (ii) _____

(iii) _____ (iv) _____

**10.** Look up the cookery terms on p. 185 of your textbook and define 'au gratin'.

_____

_____

# Eggs

**1.** Draw a labelled diagram of the structure of the egg.

2. Suggest two advantages of including eggs in the diet.

   (a) _____

   (b) _____

3. Complete the following table on the nutritive value of eggs.

| | |
|---|---|
| Type of protein | |
| Type of fat | |
| Eggs lack this nutrient | |
| Vitamins present | |
| Minerals present | |
| Percentage of water (approx) | |

4. Explain the following terms:

   (a) Free-range eggs _____

   (b) Organic eggs _____

5. (a) Illustrate the Bord Bia Quality Mark label.

   (b) What does this symbol indicate to the consumer?

   _____

   _____

6. (a) Explain what is meant by eggs curdling.

   _____

   _____

   (b) Describe two ways of preventing curdling when cooking with eggs.

      (i) _____

      (ii) _____

7. Research and suggest two examples of how eggs are used in each of the following:

| Uses | Examples |
|---|---|
| Savoury dishes | |
| Baking | |
| Coatings | |
| Glazing | |

8. Design a two-course lunch menu to include eggs as a main ingredient.

# Batters and custards

1. Explain the following terms.

   (a) Batter: _____

   _____

   (b) Custard: _____

   _____

2. (a) Give two uses for each of the following:

| Batter | Custard |
|---|---|
| | |
| | |

   (b) Identify the raising agent in a batter and explain how it is added.

   _____

   _____

   _____

   _____

# Over to you

1. Complete the crossword about milk, cheese and eggs.

## Across

5. Milk product

7. Bio yoghurts have added _____ for healthy digestive systems

9. Enzyme used in cheese production

10. Milk with added nutrients

11. Group of bacteria used in yoghurt and cheese production

12. Cream is _____ to produce butter

## Down

1. Liquid drained off in cheese production

2. Milk sugar

3. Dish made from batter

4. Type of soft cheese

6. Mixture of flour, eggs and liquid

7. Acidic milk used in baking

8. Milk in a can

2. **(a)** Research and list the ingredients in commercial custard.

   **(b)** Compare with the ingredients used to produce homemade custard.

   **(c)** Cost both products.

3. Draw a pie chart of the average composition of whole milk. Note that although all the nutrients are present, there is a very high percentage of water.

4. Draw bar charts of the average compositions of both Cheddar cheese and cottage cheese.

5. Complete the following average composition of protein foods.

| | Meat | Oily fish | Milk (whole) | Eggs | Cheese* (cheddar) |
|---|---|---|---|---|---|
| Protein | | | | | |
| Fat | | | | | |
| Carbohydrate | | | | | |
| Minerals | | | | | |
| Vitamins | | | | | |
| Water | | | | | |

\* The table should show that cheese and eggs are good substitutes for the other protein foods.

6. Examine an egg carton and find the following information:

   **(a)** The number of eggs

   **(b)** The name and the address of the supplier

   **(c)** The size of the eggs

   **(d)** The date or week number

   **(e)** The grade or class of the eggs

   **(f)** The registration number of the supplier

# Learning checklist

| | Red: **I don't know this.** Orange: **I need to study this again.** Green: **Good to go!** | ● | ● | ● |
|---|---|---|---|---|
| | I can assess the nutritive value of milk and how it contributes to health and wellbeing. | | | |
| | I appreciate why it is important to store milk correctly in the home. | | | |
| | I understand why milk is processed and can outline two methods of processing. | | | |
| | I can state different types of milk and milk products and suggest uses for each. | | | |
| | I can describe the cheese-making process. | | | |
| | I understand the nutritive value of cheese and how it contributes to health and wellbeing. | | | |
| | I can classify cheese into groups and can give examples of cheese in each group. | | | |
| | I can state some uses for cheese and I understand how cheese should be stored in the home. | | | |
| | I can outline the effects of heat on cheese. | | | |
| | I can suggest ways of increasing dairy products in the diet. | | | |
| | I can evaluate the nutritive value of eggs. | | | |
| | I can suggest some uses for eggs and how they contribute to health and wellbeing. | | | |
| | I can apply some guidelines for buying eggs and I know how eggs should be stored to avoid food waste. | | | |
| | I can make considered decisions in relation to choice of dairy products. | | | |
| | I can evaluate and compare milk, cheese, eggs and their products. | | | |

**The topic I most enjoyed in this chapter:** _____

**The topic I would like to learn more about:** _____

# Vegetables, fruit and cereals

## 11

## Vegetables

1. Vegetables are classified into four groups. Give two examples in each group.

| Roots | Greens | Fruit-vegetables | Pulses |
|---|---|---|---|
|  |  |  |  |
|  |  |  |  |

2. Which class of vegetables is most useful in a vegan diet? Explain why.

_____

_____

_____

_____

3. Explain what is meant by the term 'in season'.

_____

_____

4. Suggest two advantages of buying fruit and vegetables when they are in season.

(a) _____

(b) _____

5. Two minerals found in vegetables are calcium and iron. State the function of each.

| Mineral | Function |
|---|---|
| Calcium |  |
| Iron |  |

6. State two vitamins found in vegetables. Write down the function of each and a deficiency associated with them.

| Vitamin | Function | Deficiency |
|---|---|---|
|  |  |  |
|  |  |  |

7. Refer to the fibre content in the Food table (pp. 187–9 of your textbook). List the four best vegetable sources of fibre.

   (a) _____  (b) _____

   (c) _____  (d) _____

8. By EU law, vegetable labelling must show the following pieces of information:

   (a) _____  (b) _____  (c) _____

9. Suggest a reason for each of the following:

   (a) Weather affects the price of vegetables. _____

   (b) Buy vegetables in usable amounts. _____

   (c) Store produce in a cool place. _____

   (d) Wash fruit well before eating. _____

10. Organic vegetables are grown without artificial _____ or _____.

11. The following is a list of cooking methods.

   (a) Suggest two vegetables that could be cooked using each method:

   | Boiling | | Roasting | |
   |---|---|---|---|
   | Stir-frying | | Grilling | |
   | Steaming | | Stewing | |

   (b) Which of the above cooking methods do you consider the healthiest? Give a reason for your answer.

   | Method | Reasons |
   |---|---|
   | | |

12. Match the points given in A on the effects of cooking on vegetables with an appropriate ending in B.

   | A | B |
   |---|---|
   | Loss of vitamin C | so the texture changes. |
   | The starch cooks | so they swell. |
   | The cellulose softens | so use it for soups and sauces. |
   | Vegetables absorb water | so avoid overcooking. |
   | Minerals dissolve into the cooking liquid | so the vegetables become more digestible. |
   | Loss of colour and flavour | so eat raw when possible. |

**13.** Suggest two effects of adding butter to cooked vegetables before serving.

(a) _____

(b) _____

# Salads

**1.** State two advantages of including salads in the diet.

(a) _____

(b) _____

**2.** Suggest a suitable food that could be included in a salad in order to add:

(a) Protein _____

(b) Unsaturated fat _____

**3.** Describe how you would prepare the following salad vegetables:

(a) Lettuce _____

_____

(b) Tomato _____

_____

# Fruit

**1.** Place the following fruit into the correct class in the table below: apples, bananas, grapes, limes, nectarines, grapefruit, pears, plums, strawberries, watermelon.

| Class | Fruit |
|---|---|
| **1.** Hard | |
| **2.** Other | |
| **3.** Stone | |
| **4.** Berry | |
| **5.** Citrus | |

**2.** Complete the following sentences using the words supplied: calcium, water, fat, protein, A, iron, C, sugar.

(a) All fruits are high in _____.

(b) Fruit contains the vitamins _____ and _____ and the

minerals _____ and _____.

(c) Fruit is a good source of the carbohydrates _____ and cellulose.

(d) Fruit is lacking in _____ and _____.

**3.** Explain why fruit is useful in low-kilocalorie diets.

_____

4. Study the fibre information in the Food table on pp. 187–9 of your textbook. Identify three fruits rich in fibre.

(a) _____

(b) _____

(c) _____

5. Fruit can be used in a variety of ways in the diet. Complete the table by suggesting one example in each case.

| Use | Example |
| --- | --- |
| Desserts | Cold sweets<br>Hot puddings |
| Starters | |
| Salads | |
| Drinks | |
| Preserves | |
| Eaten raw | |
| Savoury dishes | |

6. Suggest one guideline under each heading that would help to retain the vitamin C content of fresh fruit.

| Buying | Preparing |
| --- | --- |
| | |
| | |

7. State two fruits grown in Ireland and two fruits that are imported.

| Home-grown fruits | Imported fruits |
| --- | --- |
| | |
| | |

8. Suggest two advantages of choosing locally produced fruit:

(a) _____

_____

(b) _____

_____

# Cereals

1. Cereals are the _seeds_ or _grains_ of _edible_ _grasses_ .
Examples are:

_wheat, barley, maize, oats, rice, rye_ .

2. (a) Explain what is meant by the term 'staple food' (see p. 6 of your textbook).

_Staple foods are foods that are traditionally eaten in a region. They are plentiful and_
_therefore cheaper._

(b) Suggest a reason why cereals are a staple food in many countries.

_They are cheap, filling and easy to grow in all climates._

3. Cereals supply which type or classification(s) of each of the following?

(a) Protein: _LBV Protein_

(b) Fat: _Unsaturated fat_

(c) Carbohydrates: _Starch and cellulose_

4. Cereals supply the minerals _iron_ and _calcium_ , and vitamin _B_ .

5. Indicate whether each of the following are advantages or disadvantages of including cereals in the diet.

| | Advantage | Disadvantage |
| --- | --- | --- |
| Wholegrain cereals are high in fibre. | ✓ | |
| Cereals are cheap and filling. | ✓ | |
| Cereals are high in kilocalories | | ✓ |
| Cereals may lack flavour. | | ✓ |

6. What happens when you cook cereals?

Cellulose _is softened_

Starch _becomes more digestable_

**7.** Label the diagram of a wheat grain.

A. *Starchy endosperm*

B. *bran*

C. *germ*

D. *husk*

**8.** Identify the nutrients present in each of the following.

**(a)** Bran layer: _____

**(b)** Endosperm: *starch*

**(c)** Germ: *protein, vitamin*

**9. (a)** Explain what gluten is. *a protein naturally found in many grains*

**(b)** What quality does gluten have that makes it important in bread making?

*it rises*

**10.** Cereals are sometimes 'refined'. Explain what is meant by this term.

*refined grains have been milled - bran and germ are removed*

**11. (a)** What type of wheat is used to make pasta? *durum wheat*

**(b)** Identify two other ingredients used in pasta production.

(i) *water*   (ii) *eggs*

**(c)** Name four different types of pasta.

(i) *wholegrain*

(ii) *white*

(iii) _____

(iv) _____

**12. (a)** Explain why beriberi is a common disease in countries where people eat a lot of rice.

_____

_____

_____

**(b)** What are the functions of vitamin B?

*energy release*

_____

**13.** Identify two types of rice and suggest a suitable dish for each.

| Rice | Dish |
|------|------|
| wholegrain rice | nasi goreng |
| white rice | |

**14.** Name four types of seeds and nuts that are popular in the diet.

| Seeds | Nuts |
|-------|------|
| pumpkin seeds | walnuts |
| sesame seeds | pecan nuts |
| lin seeds | almond nuts |
| poppy seeds | cashew nuts |

**15.** Suggest two advantages of including seeds and nuts in the diet.

(a) LBV protein – no saturated fat

(b) LBV protein – fibre / cellulose

**16.** Identify which cereals are used to produce the following products.

| Products | Cereal |
|----------|--------|
| Flour | wheat |
| Corn flour | corn / maize |
| Pearl barley | barley |
| Spaghetti | wheat |
| Porridge oats | |
| Popcorn | corn/maize |
| Ryvita | rye |
| Corn oil | corn/maize |

# Over to you 👉

1.  The following table shows 10 of the best fruit sources of vitamin C (per 100 g):

| Source | Vitamin C (mg) | Source | Vitamin C (mg) |
|---|---|---|---|
| Blackcurrants | 200 | Melons | 25 |
| Strawberries | 60 | Bananas | 10 |
| Oranges | 50 | Rhubarb | 10 |
| Grapefruit | 50 | Peaches | 8 |
| Raspberries | 25 | Lemons | 50 |

(a)  Represent the above information on a bar chart.

(b)  What are the functions of vitamin C?

(c)  List three other sources of vitamin C, besides fruit.

## Survey

2.  Visit a local supermarket that sells a good range of fruit and vegetables. Write a report based on the following observations:

(a)  What fresh fruit and vegetables were on sale?

(b)  Which were the more expensive items? Which were the cheapest?

(c)  Were there any fruit or vegetables in season at this particular time, but unavailable at other times of the year?

(d)  Were the fruit and vegetables nicely displayed and above ground level?

Report your findings back to the class.

3.  To check that vegetables and fruit on sale are correctly graded and labelled, visit a local vegetable shop and note your observations as in the example below.

| Vegetable | Variety | Quality | Country of origin | Cost per kg |
|---|---|---|---|---|
| Potatoes | Roosters | Class I | Ireland | |

Were there any class II fruit/vegetables on sale? Note any obvious defects/blemishes.

Note the cost per kg of five varieties of fruit and five varieties of vegetables.

# Learning checklist

**Red: I don't know this.** Orange: **I need to study this again.** Green: **Good to go!**  ● ● ●

I can classify vegetables into groups and give examples in each group.

I can assess the nutritive value of vegetables.

I understand the terms in season, organic and al dente.

I can explain how vegetables are graded and labelled for sale.

I can apply some rules when buying, storing, preparing and cooking fruit and vegetables in order to retain maximum nourishment.

I can outline the effects of cooking on vegetables.

I appreciate the value of salads in the diet and rules to follow when preparing salads.

I can classify fruit into groups and I can give examples in each class.

I can outline the nutritive value of fruit.

I can suggest some uses for fruit.

I understand how cooking and processing affect fruit.

I can suggest ways of increasing fruit and vegetable intake in the diet.

I can compare different fruit and vegetables and I can appreciate their role in maintaining health and wellbeing.

I understand the nutritive value of cereals and appreciate their role in a healthy diet.

I can draw and label the wheat grain structure and identify wheat products.

I can identify different types of rice and rice products.

I appreciate the value of nuts and seeds in the diet.

I understand how cooking affects the sensory qualities of vegetables, fruit and cereals.

**The topic I most enjoyed in this chapter:** _____

**The topic I would like to learn more about:** _____

# 12 Home baking

1. Suggest two advantages of home baking.

    (a) _usually cheaper_

    (b) _control over ingredients used_

2. Complete the following chart with examples of baking ingredients.

| Flour | wheat flour | gluten-free flour |
|-------|-------------|-------------------|
| Fat | butter | oil |
| Sugar | granulated | icing |
| Fruit | apples - fresh fruit | sultanas - dried fruit |
| Liquid | milk | water |

3. State three cereals that can be used to produce flour.

    (a) _rice_

    (b) _maize_

    (c) _wheat_

4. (a) What term is used to describe the production of flour from wheat? _milling_

    (b) Name two by-products of white-flour production.

        (i) _bran_

        (ii) _germ_

5. (a) Complete the following information on wheat flour:

| Types of wheat flour | |
|---------------------|---|
| gluten-free flour | Suitable for those with coeliac condition |
| Self-raising | white flour with added baking powder |
| strong flour | Has extra gluten |
| Wholegrain | contains the whole grain |
| white flour | Endosperm only |

**6.** Classify raising agents, giving examples.

| Class | Examples |
|---|---|
| natural | air |
| chemical | baking powder |
| biological | yeast |

**7.** Suggest two reasons for using raising agents.

(a) make bread and cakes rise

(b) make baking mixtures light and spongy

**8.** Complete the following:

(a) Acid + Alkali + Liquid = CO2

(b) Baking powder contains an acid and an alkali.

(c) Bread soda is an alkali.

(d) Buttermilk is a liquid and an acid.

**9.** Suggest a way of making milk acidic if buttermilk is unavailable.

adding lemon juice or vinegar

**10.** Explain the importance of preheating the oven when baking bread and cakes.

If the oven is underheated, the cake will be heavy and will not rise. If the oven is overheated, the cake will burn on the outside and not cook in the centre.

**11.** How do you check if the following baked products are cooked?

| Sponge cakes | cake is cooked if the surface springs back when pressed gently with a finger |
|---|---|
| Cakes | stick a skewer into the cake and if it comes out dry the cake is cooked |
| Bread | tap the bottom and if you hear a hollow sound the bread is cooked. |

**12.** Complete the following table on methods of making bread and cakes.

| Method | Used for |
|---|---|
| The rub-in method (fat rubbed into flour) | scones, yeast bread, pastry |
| creaming method: fat and sugar are creamed together at the start | Queen cakes, Madeira cakes and fruit cakes |
| All-in-one method (all ingredients placed in bowl together and beaten) | madieras queen cakes |
| whisking method: eggs and sugar are whisked together | Sponges, flans and meringues |
| Melting method (fat and sugar melted together in a saucepan) | muffins, gingerbread, boiled fruit cakes |

**13.** Research and identify the dry ingredients that are included in baking mixes.

_____

_____

_____

_____

**14.** Suggest two advantages and two disadvantages of using baking mixes.

| Advantages | Disadvantages |
|---|---|
|  |  |
|  |  |

# Pastry

**1. (a)** The basic ingredients for pastry are _____, _____ and _____.

**(b)** Richer pastries involve the addition of,_____ _____ _____.

**2.** Identify four types of pastry.

**(a)** _____

**(b)** _____

**(c)** _____

**(d)** _____

**3.** Suggest three guidelines to follow when making pastry.

**(a)** _____

**(b)** _____

**(c)** _____

**4. (a)** Explain what is meant by the term 'baking blind'.

_____

**(b)** Outline how a pastry case is baked blind.

_____

_____

_____

_____

_____

_____

_____

# Over to you

1. Find the following terms that relate to baking in the word search.

ACID      CHOUX      GERM      SCONES
ADDITIVES      COELIAC      GLUTEN      SPONGE
ALKALI      CREAMING      MELTING      WHEAT
BRAN      FILO      OATS      WHISKING
BREAD      FLAKY      PRESERVATIVES      YEAST

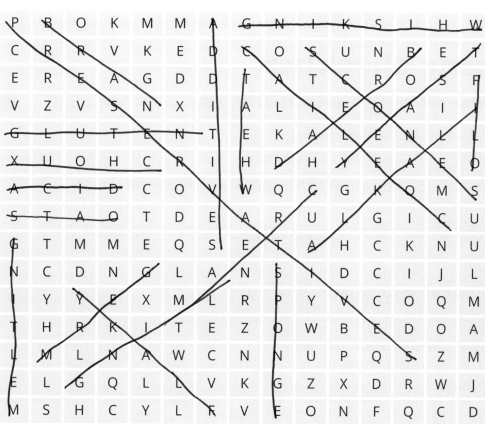

2. Design a chart of the guidelines to follow when baking. Display it in the Home Economics room.

3. Visit a local supermarket and investigate the different baking mixes available and complete the following table.

| Baking mixes | Cost | Weight |
| --- | --- | --- |
| | | |
| | | |
| | | |
| | | |
| | | |

**4. (a)** Research and investigate examples of dishes that use the following types of pastry:

(i) Shortcrust pastry

(ii) Flaky pastry

(iii) Choux pastry

(iv) Rough puff pastry

(v) Filo pastry

(b) Prepare, cook and serve a sweet or savoury dish using shortcrust pastry.

# Learning checklist

| Red: I don't know this. Orange: I need to study this again. Green: Good to go! | ● | ● | ● |
|---|---|---|---|
| I appreciate the advantages of home baking. | | | |
| I understand the ingredients required and the guidelines for baking at home. | | | |
| I can explain how the different raising agents work. | | | |
| I can describe the methods of making bread and cakes. | | | |
| I can use and evaluate commercial baking mixes. | | | |
| I can compare and evaluate homemade and commercial baked products. | | | |

**The topic I most enjoyed in this chapter:** _____

**The topic I would like to learn more about:** _____

# Food shopping **13**

1. What are the three most important points to consider when:

   (a) Choosing where to shop for food: _____

   _____

   _____

   (b) Planning your shopping: _____

   _____

   _____

2. Explain what this symbol indicates (see p. 151 in your textbook).

   _____

   _____

   _____

   FAIRTRADE

3. Explain the benefits to the consumer of:

   (a) Own-brand goods _____

   (b) Keeping a receipt _____

4. Suggest two ways to be environmentally aware when shopping.

   (a) _____

   (b) _____

5. State one reason why shops do the following:

   (a) Place essentials at the back of the shop

   _____

   (b) Bake bread on the premises

   _____

   (c) Place heavy goods at the entrance

   _____

   (d) Place magazines at the checkout

   _____

# Convenience foods and processed foods

1. State two examples of each of the following convenience foods.

| Groups | Examples |
|---|---|
| Frozen food | |
| Tinned / bottled food | |
| Dried food | |
| Cook-chill foods | |
| Ready-to-cook meals | |

2. Identify an example of a food to match each of the following reasons for processing food.

To increase the shelf life of food: _____

To make sure the food stays safe to eat: _____

To make new food products: _____

To fortify some foods: _____

To save time and energy when preparing food: _____

3. Identify three reasons why convenience foods are so popular.

(a) _____

(b) _____

(c) _____

4. Give two advantages and two disadvantages of including convenience foods in the diet.

| Advantages | Disadvantages |
|---|---|
| | |
| | |

5. State one advantage of frozen food over each of the following:

(a) Tinned food _____

(b) Dried food _____

6. Suggest one advantage of tinned food over each of the following:

(a) Dried food _____

(b) Frozen food _____

**7.** State one point in each case for the safe handling of cook-chill foods.

| Buying | Storing | Using |
|---|---|---|
| | | |
| | | |

**8.** List one rule in each case for the safe handling of tinned food.

| Buying | Storing | Using |
|---|---|---|
| | | |
| | | |

# Additives

**1.** Define an additive. _____

_____

**2.** Suggest three reasons why additives might be present in food.

(a) _____

(b) _____

(c) _____

**3.** Complete the following table:

| Additive | Example | Function |
|---|---|---|
| Colouring | | |
| | | To improve taste |
| | Lecithin | |
| Antioxidants | | |
| | Vitamin B | |
| | | Sweeten low calorie drinks |
| | Vinegar | |

**4.** Explain the following terms and give an example of each:

| | Definition | Example |
|---|---|---|
| Fortified food | | |
| Functional food | | |

**5.** Suggest two advantages and two disadvantages of using additives in food.

| | Using additives in food | |
|---|---|---|
| Advantages | | |
| Disadvantages | | |

# Packaging

**1. (a)** Identify two examples of foods that are sold packaged in each of the following materials:

| Paper | Plastic | Metal | Glass |
|---|---|---|---|
| | | | |
| | | | |

**(b)** State one advantage and one disadvantage of each form of packaging.

| Paper | Plastic | Metal | Glass |
|---|---|---|---|
| Advantage | Advantage | Advantage | Advantage |
| | | | |
| Disadvantage | Disadvantage | Disadvantage | Disadvantage |
| | | | |

**2.** Identify a packaging material that is:

**(a)** Biodegradable _____

**(b)** Recyclable _____

**3.** Identify the four qualities that you think are most important in food packaging.

**(a)** _____

**(b)** _____

**(c)** _____

**(d)** _____

**4.** Many foods are over packed. State two disadvantages of a food product having too much packaging material.

**(a)** _____

**(b)** _____

**5.** What information does this symbol give the consumer?

_____

_____

# Food labelling

1. Suggest two reasons why labelling on food products is necessary.

   (a) _____

   (b) _____

2. State six pieces of information found on a tin of baked beans.

   (a) _____  (b) _____

   (c) _____  (d) _____

   (e) _____  (f) _____

3. Outline why detailed ingredient lists are essential on food products.

   _____

   _____

   _____

4. (a) Explain what is meant by the term 'date stamping'.

   _____

   (b) Suggest two reasons why it is important to observe date stamps on food.

   (i) _____

   (ii) _____

5. State two examples of foods that could carry each of the following date stamps:

| Foods | | |
|---|---|---|
| Use by | | |
| Best before | | |

6. Explain the following terms (see pp. 65–6 of your textbook).

   (a) Shelf life: _____

   _____

   (b) Perishable: _____

   _____

7. (a) What is meant by the term 'unit pricing'?

   _____

   (b) List two foods that are unit priced.

   (i) _____  (ii) _____

   (c) Explain how unit pricing benefits the consumer. _____

   _____

8. (a) Explain what the purpose of a bar code is. _____

_____

(b) Suggest two advantages of bar coding for the consumer.

(i) _____

(ii) _____

# Over to you 👆

1. The labels A, B and C are from the following foods:

   - Marmalade
   - Breakfast cereal
   - A white sauce mix

   (a) Can you match the product to the label?

   (b) The products are all very different, yet they all have one ingredient in common. Name that ingredient. Would you consider that ingredient necessary in the sauce mix?

   (c) List the two main ingredients in each product. Is there anything surprising about these?

   (d) One of the products is 'fortified' with vitamins. Name the product and list the vitamins added. Explain the term 'fortified'.

**A**

Oat bran, wheat, sugar, glycerated raisins, apple, glucose syrup, salt, malt Riboflavin (B2), Thiamine (B1), folic acid, Vitamin D, Vitamin B12

**B**

Wheat flour, salt, hydrogenated vegetable oil, bouillon powder, flavour enhancer (sodium glutamate), dried whey, dried skimmed milk, dried onion, cream solids, mustard flour, sugar, spices (mace, celery, black pepper, nutmeg)

**C**

Sugar, glucose syrup, oranges, gelling agent, pectin, citric acid, acidity, regulator, sodium citrate acid, acidity, regulator, sodium citrate

2. Choose a label from any prepacked food and complete the following chart:

| Type of food/ Brand name | Date stamp | Storage instructions | Nutritional information |
|---|---|---|---|
|  |  |  |  |
| **Additives** | **Weight** | **Ingredients** | **Special claims** |
|  |  |  |  |
| **Name of packer/ producer** | **Bar code** | **Instructions for use** | **Any other information** |
|  |  |  |  |

3. Research the cost of the following products: tea, coffee, flour, milk, baked beans, butter.

   Calculate the cost per 100 g or 100 ml.

**4.** Examine the case study below.

## Case study

Katie is a young office worker who lives independently.  She usually does her grocery shopping on her way home from work when she is tired and hungry.  She buys a lot of processed and convenience foods for her dinner and for lunch the next day.  She is often surprised at the cost and knows that she has to make some changes.

(a)  Suggest some steps that Katie should take in order to eat healthily while staying within her budget.

(b)  Suggest some economical main course dishes that Katie should consider including in her diet. Write a shopping list for one of these dishes.

# Learning checklist

**Red: I don't know this.** Orange: **I need to study this again.** Green: **Good to go!**  ● ● ●

I know what to consider when choosing a food shop and a supermarket.

I appreciate the need for planning when shopping for food.

I can suggest some guidelines to follow when shopping.

I can apply sustainable practices when shopping for food.

I am aware of techniques used to increase sales.

I can define convenience foods and identify why food is processed.

I can identify some advantages and disadvantages of convenience foods.

I can evaluate different types of convenience foods.

I can interpret information on food labels.

I can appreciate the need to combine convenience foods with fresh foods.

I can compare commercial products with homemade products in terms of nutrition and value for money.

I can define the term 'additive' and I know why additives are used in food.

I can state different types of additives and give examples of their use in food.

I can explain what is meant by fortified and functional foods and I can give an example of each.

I appreciate the need for some food packaging.

I can compare and evaluate the different types of packaging materials.

I understand why labelling is so important.

I can identify some information found on prepacked foods.

I understand what date stamping, unit pricing and bar codes mean.

**The topic I most enjoyed in this chapter:** _____

**The topic I would like to learn more about:** _____

# 14 Food sustainability

## Convenience foods

**1. (a)** Explain what is meant by sustainability. _____

_____

**(b)** Food sustainability involves choosing foods that do not harm the _____,

_____ or _____.

**2.** State one benefit for the environment in each case:

**(a)** Buying locally produced food

_____

**(b)** Reducing food waste in the home

_____

**(c)** Buying Fairtrade products

_____

**(d)** Choosing organically produced food

_____

**3.** Define food miles. _____

**4.** Match the figure for food waste in column A with a suitable example in column B.

| A | B |
|---|---|
| 80 kg | Food going to waste in Ireland |
| 300,000 tonnes | Food waste that cannot be avoided |
| 20% | Amount of food waste per person in Ireland |

**5.** Almost 25% of fruit and vegetables are thrown out. What could you do at home in order to prevent this food waste?

_____

_____

**6.** How do children in poorer countries benefit from 'Fairtrade'?

_____

_____

# Leftovers

1.  Suggest two guidelines to follow when using leftover meat in order to prevent food poisoning.

    (a) _____

    (b) _____

2.  How can the following characteristics be added to reheated foods?

    (a) Colour: _____

    (b) Flavour: _____

    (c) Texture: _____

3.  Suggest a different dish in which you would use each of the following leftover foods:

| Leftovers | Dishes |
|---|---|
| Roast chicken | |
| Mashed potato | |
| Half tin of tomatoes | |

# Food preservation

1.  Food spoilage is caused by: _____ and _____.

2.  Identify four conditions required for the growth of microorganisms.

    (a) _____        (b) _____

    (c) _____        (d) _____

3.  What growth condition of microorganisms is removed by each of the following?

| Refrigeration | Drying | Canning | Good hygiene practices |
|---|---|---|---|
| | | | |

4.  Suggest an example of a suitable food for each method of preservation.

| Method | Example |
|---|---|
| Canning | |
| Pasteurisation | |
| Irradiation | |
| Freeze drying | |

**5.** Give two reasons why preserving food is considered to be sustainable.

(a) _____

(b) _____

**6. (a)** Draw the irradiated food symbol.

    **(b)** Explain how irradiation preserves food.

_____

_____

_____

_____

# Freezing

**1.** Explain why microorganisms are inactivated by freezing.

_____

_____

**2.** Home freezing is done at _____ to _____ degrees C.

Blast freezing is done at _____ degrees C.

**3. (a)** List four packaging materials that are suitable for use in a freezer.

    (i) _____

    (ii) _____

    (iii) _____

    (iv) _____

    **(b)** Suggest two packaging materials that are unsuitable for use in a freezer.

    (i) _____

    (ii) _____

**4.** Give one reason for each of the following.

    **(a)** Using moisture-proof containers: _____

    **(b)** Freezing food in usable quantities: _____

    **(c)** Labelling and dating each food before freezing: _____

**5.** Explain the term 'blanching'.

_____

_____

_____

_____

6. Describe how to freeze carrots under the following headings:

| Preparation | Packaging | Freezing | Storing |
| --- | --- | --- | --- |
|  |  |  |  |

7. Complete the table for frozen foods.

| Food | Suitable packaging | Storage time |
| --- | --- | --- |
| Beef casserole |  |  |
| Apple tart |  |  |
| Uncooked salmon |  |  |
| Vegetable soup |  |  |
| Peas |  |  |

# Jam making

1. Outline how making jam prevents food spoilage.

_____

_____

_____

2. Complete the following sentences.

   Pectin is a type of _____ found in _____ that helps jam to _____.

   Jam sugar has added _____. Fruits may be combined to ensure sufficient _____.

3. Describe one test that can be used in order to see if the setting point of a jam has been reached.

   _____

   _____

   _____

   _____

   _____

   _____

   _____

   _____

# Over to you 👆

1. Unscramble the following methods of preservation in the table below.

| | Methods of preservation |
|---|---|
| Ezefr gdnriy | |
| Mja kimagn | |
| Notiirasasptue | |
| Gnnnica | |
| Gferezni | |
| Iadrairnito | |
| Ringdy | |

2. (a) Visit a local supermarket to conduct a survey:
   - Which Irish-produced vegetables and fruit are on sale?
   - Is any of the produce grown in your locality?
   - Are there imported vegetables or fruit on sale? What is their country of origin?
   - Note six fruits or vegetables that are prepacked. Note six that are sold loosely.
   - Note any organic produce on offer. Is it more expensive than other produce?
   - What 'Fairtrade' goods are available? Are they more or less expensive than other brands?
   - Are there 'free-range' eggs or chickens on sale? Note the price. Are they more expensive?

   (b) On a separate sheet of paper write a report of your findings and present it to the class.

3. Plan and present a menu for a three-course dinner party, choosing courses that could be cooked in advance and then frozen until required.

4.
## Activity

Try making your own jam. Use the recipe in your textbook (see p. 182) or find your own recipe.

Compare the jam with a similar commercial product using the comparison sheet B on p. 101.

# Learning checklist

**Red: I don't know this.** Orange: **I need to study this again.** Green: **Good to go!**

| | ● | ● | ● |
|---|---|---|---|
| I can explain what is meant by food sustainability. | | | |
| I can apply sustainable practices in the choice and use of foods. | | | |
| I understand the benefits of choosing locally produced food. | | | |
| I can apply my knowledge to prevent food waste in my selection and management of food. | | | |
| I understand the ethical benefits of Fairtrade products. | | | |
| I can suggest some rules for safely storing and using leftover food. | | | |
| I can state some advantages and disadvantages of using leftover food. | | | |
| I understand what is meant by food preservation. | | | |
| I can state some advantages of preserving food. | | | |
| I can outline some methods of preservation. | | | |
| I appreciate that freezing and jam making are methods of home preservation that contribute to food sustainability. | | | |
| I understand how to test jam for setting. | | | |
| I can make informed and ethical decisions when buying and using food. | | | |

**The topic I most enjoyed in this chapter:** _____

**The topic I would like to learn more about:** _____

# 15 Digestion

1. **(a)** Explain what is meant by digestion. _____.

   **(b)** Where does digestion take place? _____.

2. Distinguish between physical and chemical changes that occur during digestion.

   **(a)** Physical changes: _____

   **(b)** Chemical changes: _____

3. Identify two physical/mechanical changes that food goes through during digestion.

   **(a)** _____

   **(b)** _____

4. The chemicals involved in digestion are called _____.

5. The digestive enzyme in the mouth is _____; it breaks down _____.

6. **(a)** Which three nutrients require chemical breakdown?

   **(i)** _____

   **(ii)** _____

   **(iii)** _____

   **(b)** Which three nutrients do not require chemical breakdown?

   **(i)** _____

   **(ii)** _____

   **(iii)** _____

7. Complete the following chemical changes:

   **(a)** Proteins are broken down into _____.

   **(b)** Carbohydrates are broken down into _____.

   **(c)** Fats are broken down into _____ and _____.

# The digestive system

1. **(a)** What physical breakdown occurs in the mouth?

   _____

   **(b)** What chemical breakdown occurs in the mouth?

   _____

2. Describe what is meant by peristalsis.

_____

_____

_____

3. Complete the following sentences:

Food is _____ in the stomach. The digestive juice of the stomach is called _____

juice. It contains _____ acid and enzymes. The hydrochloric acid kills _____.

The enzymes break down _____.

4. Describe the functions of each of the following digestive juices.

   (a) Bile: _____

   (b) Pancreatic juice: _____

   (c) Intestinal juice: _____

5. (a) What is meant by absorption? _____

   (b) Absorption occurs mainly in the _____.

6. (a) What are villi? _____

   (b) Where are villi located in the digestive system?_____

   (c) What is their function? _____

   _____

7. Outline the functions of the large intestine.

_____

_____

_____

_____

8. Complete the following sentences:

   (a) The waste eliminated from the body is known as _____.

   (b) A diet high in _____ helps waste elimination.

9. Identify six important dietary sources of fibre.

   (a) _____

   (b) _____

   (c) _____

   (d) _____

   (e) _____

   (f) _____

**10.** Label the diagram of the digestive system.

A.  _____

B.  _____

C.  _____

D.  _____

E.  _____

F.  _____

G.  _____

H.  _____

I.  _____

**11.** Insert the missing words into the following paragraphs.

Food goes into the _____ and is broken up into small pieces by the _____.
The digestive enzyme in the mouth is called _____.

It breaks down starch. The food then moves into the _____ and moves along

by _____. A juice called the _____ is produced by the inner wall of the

stomach. _____ acid is also present in the stomach.

Because of the heat in the stomach, fat _____. The food then moves into the

small _____. Two digestive juices enter the small intestine: _____ and

_____ juice. _____ is emulsified by bile and the juice of the pancreas

continues the digestion of the nutrients. The _____ juice completes the digestion

of the nutrients.

Tiny hair-like projections called _____ line the inside wall of the small intestine.
It is through these that the digested food is _____. Waste is then passed into the

_____ _____ where water is _____. Vitamins B and

_____ are manufactured here. Waste called _____ is expelled

from the body.

# Over to you ☞

1. Discuss each of the following and indicate if the statement is true or false.

| Statement | True | False |
|---|:---:|:---:|
| Digestion is the breakdown of food. | ○ | ○ |
| Enzymes are chemicals that break down food during digestion. | ○ | ○ |
| Amylase breaks down fats in the mouth. | ○ | ○ |
| Proteins are broken down into simple sugars in digestion. | ○ | ○ |
| Food flows into the liver and pancreas during digestion. | ○ | ○ |
| Bile is produced in the pancreas. | ○ | ○ |
| Villi are tiny hair-like projections in the small intestine. | ○ | ○ |
| Food is mostly absorbed through the stomach. | ○ | ○ |
| Absorption is the passing of digested nutrients into the bloodstream. | ○ | ○ |
| Vitamins A and D are produced in the large intestine. | ○ | ○ |

2. Draw a poster of a labelled diagram of the digestive system and display it in the classroom.

# Learning checklist

| Red: **I don't know this.** Orange: **I need to study this again.** Green: **Good to go!** | ● | ● | ● |
|---|---|---|---|
| I can describe the basic structure and functions of the digestive system. | | | |
| I can explain the term 'digestion'. | | | |
| I can distinguish between the physical and the chemical changes that happen to food during digestion. | | | |
| I can state an enzyme involved in digestion and the nutrient on which it works. | | | |
| I can draw and label the diagram of the digestive system. | | | |
| I can explain how digested food is absorbed into the bloodstream. | | | |

**The topic I most enjoyed in this chapter:** _____

**The topic I would like to learn more about:** _____

# 16 Recipes and culinary skills

1. Suggest a suitable dish or product for a healthy family meal.

   Starter/soup: _____

   Main course: _____

   Dessert: _____

2. Suggest a suitable dish or product for a healthy snack for the following people.

   (a) A three-year-old child: _____

   (b) A school-going teenager: _____

   (c) A woman who wishes to lose weight: _____

   (d) An elderly man: _____

3. Suggest a suitable dish or product for a healthy packed lunch for the following people.

   (a) A child: _____

   (b) A manual worker: _____

4. Suggest a suitable dish or product for a main course meal for people on special diets.

   (a) An obese person who wishes to lose weight: _____

   (b) A vegan: _____

   (c) Someone on a low-cholesterol diet: _____

   (d) Someone with coeliac disease: _____

   (e) A diabetic: _____

   (f) Someone on a high-fibre diet: _____

5. Suggest a suitable dish or product for a main course meal for the following people.

   (a) A child: _____

   (b) A teenager: _____

   (c) A manual worker: _____

   (d) A pregnant woman: _____

   (e) An elderly person: _____

6. Suggest two dishes that can be modified as a healthy alternative to a commercial or takeaway meal.

   (a) _____   (b) _____

7. Suggest four food products suitable for a farmers' market.

   (a) _____   (b) _____

   (c) _____   (d) _____

8. Suggest three dishes that could be made using leftovers.

   (a) _____ (b) _____ (c) _____

9. Identify three countries and a staple dish associated with each country, which could be made in a practical class.

   (a) _____

   (b) _____

   (c) _____

10. (a) Explain what is meant by modifying a recipe. _____

    _____

    (b) Suggest two reasons why a recipe might be modified.

       (i) _____

       (ii) _____

11. Examine each of the modifications to the pizza recipe on p. 183 of your textbook. In each case, explain how the modification makes the pizza more nutritious.

    (a) _____

    (b) _____

    (c) _____

    (d) _____

12. Look up the ingredients for the following recipes in your textbook. Suggest two modifications for each to make them more nourishing and in keeping with healthy eating guidelines.

    (a) Quiche, see p. 174 in your textbook.

       (i) _____ (ii) _____

    (b) Apple and blueberry crumble, see p. 175 in your textbook.

       (i) _____ (ii) _____

    (c) Spaghetti Bolognese, see p. 168 in your textbook.

       (i) _____ (ii) _____

13. Explain the difference between the terms 'garnishing' and 'decorating' a dish. _____

    _____

14. Look up the cookery terms on p. 185 of your textbook. Explain the following food preparation terms.

    (a) Beat/whisk: _____

    (b) Dice: _____

    (c) Knead: _____

    (d) Sauté: _____

    (e) Glaze: _____

# Product comparison sheet A

## Comparing a range of products

Date: _____ Product: _____

Complete the product comparison sheets using the descriptors on p. 184 in your textbook.

| Product | A | B | C | D |
|---|---|---|---|---|
| Brand name | | | | |
| Appearance and colour | | | | |
| Flavour | | | | |
| Texture | | | | |
| Nutritive value | | | | |

**Preferred product:** _____

**Reasons:** _____

_____

_____

# Product comparison sheet B

## Homemade product versus commercial product

Product: _____

|  | A: Homemade product | B: Commercial product |
|---|---|---|
| Main ingredients |  |  |
| Additives |  |  |
| Cost |  |  |
| Serving size |  |  |
| Cost per serving |  |  |

Indicate which product you prefer in terms of:

- Appearance and colour: _____
- Flavour: _____
- Texture: _____

Which product do you think is most nutritious? _____

Preferred product: _____

Using the descriptors on p. 184 of your textbook give reasons why you prefer this product.

_____

# Classroom-based assessment 2 and the practical exam

## Sample tasks

### First Year sample tasks

1. Prepare, cook and serve a snack suitable for a lunchbox for a teenager.
2. Prepare, cook and serve a breakfast main course dish.
3. Prepare, cook and serve a dessert using a variety of fresh fruit.
4. Prepare, cook and serve a dish suitable for lunch or tea.
5. Make two batches of 200 g of shortcrust pastry. Freeze one and use the other to make a pastry dish.
6. Prepare a sweet dish suitable for a child's birthday party.
7. Using a variety of fresh vegetables, prepare, cook and serve a soup of your choice.
8. Make a simple cake to serve for afternoon tea.

### Second Year sample tasks

1. Research, prepare, cook and serve savoury scones. Compare the cost of homemade scones with commercial scones.
2. Research, prepare, cook and serve a savoury dish that includes a roux sauce.
3. Design a two-course dinner menu for a family to include a main course meat dish. Prepare, cook and serve the main course.
4. Make a sweet pastry dish using commercial frozen pastry.
5. Design a two-course menu to include fresh or smoked fish, or chicken, in the main course. Prepare, cook and serve the dish.
6. Design a two-course menu suitable for a vegan or lacto-vegetarian. Prepare, cook and serve the main course dish.
7. Prepare and serve two tasty salads.
8. Prepare, cook and serve a batch of biscuits.
9. Research, prepare cook and serve a selection of savoury and sweet dishes suitable for a buffet for a special occasion.

# Third Year sample tasks

1. Current dietary guidelines recommend that we should increase our intake of fresh fruit and vegetables.

   (a) Research the value of fruit and vegetables in the diet.

   (b) Using digital technology, source recipes and design a three-course family meal to reflect current healthy eating guidelines. Include dishes that contain a variety of fresh fruit and vegetables.

   (c) Prepare, cook and serve two of the courses.

   (d) Cost the complete meal.

2. Certain people have special dietary needs.

   (a) Using digital technology, research two of these dietary needs.

   (b) Design a two-course menu suitable for an evening meal for one of the conditions you investigated.

   (c) Prepare, cook and serve the complete main course of the meal.

   (d) Evaluate the meal in terms of nutritional suitability.

   (e) Prepare and serve the starter or the dessert to complete the evening meal.

3. Young athletes need to eat a balanced diet to maintain good health and achieve peak performance.

   (a) Research and outline the benefits of omega-3 fatty acids in the diet of young athletes.

   (b) Using a suitable app, source recipes and design a two-course dinner menu for athletes that includes fresh fish or smoked fish, or chicken, as a key ingredient.

   (c) Demonstrate your skills by preparing, cooking and serving the complete main course of the meal suitable for at least two athletes.

   (d) Prepare an attractive salad and a simple dressing to serve with the meal.

4. A large variety of commercial and takeaway meals are available.

   (a) Research a selection of these meals.

   (b) Using a suitable app, source a recipe or modify a recipe for a healthy homemade alternative.

   (c) Prepare and cook the meal. Serve in suitable sustainable packaging.

   (d) Cost the meal and compare with a similar commercial meal.

5. Using digital technology research products suitable for a food enterprise or farmers' market.

   (a) Choosing a baked product, demonstrate your culinary skills by preparing and baking a batch of your chosen product.

   (b) Choose a suitable sustainable packaging material and design an attractive label for your product to include a brief account of the nutritional value of your product.

   (c) Calculate the cost per portion of the product and estimate retail price to ensure a reasonable profit.

# Home Economics self-assessment

Date _____ Task no. _____ Dish/es _____

| Preparation | Yes | No |
|---|---|---|
| I read the task carefully. | | |
| I studied the recipe/work plan <u>before</u> the practical class. | | |
| I brought all the ingredients I needed to make the dish. | | |
| I weighed and measured all ingredients accurately. | | |
| I remembered to bring a container to take home food. | | |

I will improve my preparation by: _____

😃 I did it very well          🙂 I could have done it better          🙁 I did not do it at all

| Practical class | 😃 | 🙂 | 🙁 |
|---|---|---|---|
| 1. I prepared myself first, i.e. I tied back my hair, washed my hands and put on an apron. | | | |
| 2. I collected all the equipment I needed and set up the table correctly. | | | |
| 3. I preheated the oven to the correct temperature. | | | |
| 4. I lined the bin with a plastic bag. | | | |
| 5. I worked well following my recipe/work plan. | | | |
| 6. I did not waste any food or ingredients. | | | |
| 7. I followed all the rules of safety and hygiene. | | | |
| 8. I did my wash-up in a neat and logical order. | | | |
| 9. I kept a close eye on the food as it cooked. | | | |
| 10. I served up the finished dish attractively. | | | |

I can improve my practical work by:

_____

Signed _____

# Strand 1 review
## In this strand, you learned about:

- Food choices
- Nutrition
- Balanced eating
- Special diets
- Meal planning

- Food safety and hygiene
- Food preparation
- Cooking food
- Food commodities

- Home baking
- Food shopping
- Food sustainability
- Digestion
- Recipes and culinary skills

Look back over the topics covered in Strand 1. On the table below, identify (tick) which of the skills you have used as you worked through Strand 1 **Food, health and culinary skills**.

| Managing myself | Staying well | Managing information and thinking | 1,2,3... Being numerate |
|---|---|---|---|
| I know more about myself. ○ | I am more aware of being healthy and active. ○ | I am curious. ○ | I expressed ideas mathematically. ○ |
| I made considered decisions. ○ | I am social. ○ | I gathered and analysed information. ○ | I estimated, predicted and calculated. ○ |
| I set and achieved goals. ○ | I feel safe. ○ | I thought creatively and critically. ○ | I was interested in problem-solving. ○ |
| I reflected on my learning. ○ | I am spiritual. ○ | I reflected on and evaluated my learning. ○ | I saw patterns, trends and relationships. ○ |
| I made use of technology in my learning. ○ | I feel confident. ○ | I used digital technology to access, manage and share information. ○ | I gathered, analysed and presented data. ○ |
| | I feel positive about what I learned. ○ | | I used digital technology to develop numeracy skills and understanding. ○ |
| | I am responsible, safe and ethical in using digital technology. ○ | | |

| Being creative | Working with others | Communicating | abc Being literate |
|---|---|---|---|
| I used my imagination. ○ | I developed good relationships. ○ | I used language. ○ | I developed my language skills. ○ |
| I explored options and alternatives. ○ | I dealt with conflict. ○ | I used numbers. ○ | I enjoyed words and language. ○ |
| I put ideas into action. ○ | I co-operated with others while respecting difference. ○ | I listened to my classmates. ○ | I wrote for different purposes. ○ |
| I learned in a creative way. ○ | I helped make the world a better place. ○ | I expressed myself. ○ | I expressed my ideas clearly and accurately. ○ |
| I was creative with digital technology. ○ | I learned with others. ○ | I performed/ presented. ○ | I developed my spoken language. ○ |
| | I worked with others using digital technology. ○ | I had a discussion/ debate. ○ | I read and wrote in different ways. ○ |
| | | I used technology to communicate. ○ | |

# 18 The family

1. Define the term 'family'.

   a group of people related to each other by blood, marraige or other special connection like adoption. ✓

2. Describe each of these family types.

   Nuclear family: parents and child/children ✓

   Extended family: nuclear family and grandparents, cosins, etc. aunts and uncles

   One-parent families: parent and child/children ✓

   Blended family: 2 adults who had previous relationships and make a new family ✓

3. Social, cultural and economic factors all influence family life. Give examples of each:

   | Social | Cultural | Economic |
   |---|---|---|
   | • how many parents<br>• number of children<br>• ~~Marraige~~<br>• marraige | • family background<br>• race and religion<br>• local tradition<br>• peer pressure | • wealthy/poorer<br>• employed/unemployed<br>• money spent on childcare, health care, etc. |

4. Identify three functions of the family.

   (a) physical support ✓  — food

   (b) emotional guidance/support ✓  — understand

   (c) educational support ✓  — ~~~~ teach, homework

5. Place the examples of physical, emotional and social needs in the correct circle.

   **Physical needs**
   Food
   Clothing
   Protection

   **Emotional needs**
   Safe environment
   Love
   Protection

   **Social needs**
   Social Skill
   Being an effective communicator

   Social skill
   Love

   Safe environment
   Being an effective communicator

   Food
   Clothing
   Protection

**6.** Identify the type of child development in each case:

**(a)** Learning good manners

Social development

**(b)** Getting taller

Physical development

**(c)** Learning how to deal with disappointment

Emotional development

**7.** State three rights of children and three rights of adults.

| Rights of children | Rights of adults |
|---|---|
| Love and understanding | to work |
| Education | to vote |
| Protection from cruelty and neglect | to consumer rights |

**8.** Define each of the terms set out in this table.

| Right | Role | Responsibility |
|---|---|---|
| something that a person is entitled to | the way we are expected to behave in life | something for which a person is answerable |

**9.** Fill in two examples of responsibilities for each of the following:

| Child | Adolescent | Adult |
|---|---|---|
| to show respect for others | to be cooperative and dependable at home | to provide for their children's needs |
| to learn how to behave in society | to participate well in school | to help children develop life skills |

**10.** Outline two roles of the parents within a family.

**(a)** caring for the needs of their children

**(b)** providing financially for children

**11.** Explain the following terms.

**(a)** Gender roles: ~~learned by observing the world around us - e.g our parents, our environment, the media~~ how you are supposed to behave based on your gender

**(b)** Gender equity: the equal treatment of males and females

**(c)** Gender inequality: when males or females are treated unfairly

**12.** Suggest one effect of gender inequality. Gender stereotyping: for example the idea that women should stay at home and do housework while men go out and work.

13. (a) Stereotyping is _seeing things, people or groups in a certain, preconcieved way_ ✓

    (b) An example of stereotyping is: _all Irish people drink too much alchohol .._

14. Explain the following terms.

    (a) Norm: _an acceptable way of behaving in society_ ✓

    (b) Relationship: _an interaction between people_ ✓

15. Outline three relationships that exist within the family.

    (a) _Parent - child relationships: children should be able to trust their parents, parents are responsible for teaching their children right and wrong_

    (b) _mother - father: close and loving, parents sharing equal responsibility for the family_

    (c) _Sibling: close and caring relationships, equal treatment by parents_

16. (a) Communication is _how we relate to one another_

    (b) Differentiate between verbal and nonverbal commication giving two examples of each.

    _verbal: anything with words, eg talking, texting_

    _non verbal: an communication without words, eg evil eye, smiling_

17. List three characteristics of a good communicator.

    (a) _Listening attentively_

    (b) _Speaking clearly_

    (c) _Looking people in the eye_

18. Suggest three causes of conflict between teenagers and parents.

    (a) _Teenagers questioning the rules_

    (b) _Teenagers looking for more freedom which may lead to schoolwork and study suffering_

    (c) _Social media and other influences such as peer pressure and boyfriend/girlfriend relationships_

**19.** Recommend three ways of dealing with conflict.

(a) ___trying to understand how the other person feels___

(b) ___compromising - give and take - is the best way to solve conflict___

(c) ___good communication is essential to deal with conflict___

# Over to you

**1.** Complete the word search about families.

| BLENDED | FAMILY | RELATIONSHIP |
| COMMUNICATION | GENDER | RESPONSIBILITY |
| CONFLICT | NORM | ROLE |
| EXTENDED | PEER | |

| B | U | N | X | X | G | H | T | G | J | Q | S | F | X | P |
|---|---|---|---|---|---|---|---|---|---|---|---|---|---|---|
| D | L | J | O | E | X | T | E | N | D | E | D | A | O | I |
| J | T | E | N | I | T | E | O | Q | E | X | N | M | O | H |
| R | F | D | N | S | T | T | D | T | T | G | N | I | R | S |
| T | E | M | M | D | H | A | C | U | C | P | C | L | E | N |
| R | V | E | G | Z | E | I | C | E | H | T | F | Y | P | O |
| R | S | U | P | M | L | D | M | I | I | N | E | E | C | I |
| R | N | U | N | F | Y | M | B | P | N | H | U | G | U | T |
| E | M | B | N | E | D | N | Z | G | N | U | Q | X | B | A |
| L | P | O | D | N | B | J | Y | Z | K | O | M | B | A | L |
| O | C | I | V | L | R | L | O | A | U | P | R | M | D | E |
| R | H | S | T | A | I | X | O | Q | S | F | L | V | O | R |
| Y | T | I | L | I | B | I | S | N | O | P | S | E | R | C |
| M | R | O | N | W | A | M | N | R | F | L | L | V | F | G |
| V | J | O | Q | R | I | O | Y | T | Y | H | M | O | S | Q |

2. Break the stereotypes! Think of examples of how boys and girls do not follow the gender stereotype. The first example is given to get you started.

(a) A girl boxes in her local gym.

(b) <u>A boy takes dance classes</u>

(c) <u>A girl who plays rugby</u>

(d) <u>A boy who sews</u>

(e) <u>A father who stays at home</u>

3. Suggest how you might resolve these conflicts.

| Example | Solution |
|---|---|
| Girls in your class are making fun of you for being tall. | |
| Your friends dare you to drink some beer but you do not want to. | communication – say clearly that you do not want to but you don't mind if they do |
| Your parents are giving out to you for being on your phone all the time. | compromise with a set amount of screen time |
| You get into a big argument with your best friend because they say you are spending too much time with your boyfriend. | listen to what they say and compromise by organising to meet up with your friend |

# Learning checklist

| Red: I don't know this. Orange: I need to study this again. Green: Good to go! | ● | ● | ● |
|---|---|---|---|
| I can describe different types of families and list some factors that influence family life. | | | |
| I can state the functions of the family. | | | |
| I can identify the basic needs of children and adolescents. | | | |
| I understand what is meant by rights, responsibilities and roles and I can give examples of each for children, teenagers and parents. | | | |
| I can describe some family relationships and I understand the importance of good family communication. | | | |
| I can identify causes of conflict between parents and teenagers and I can recommend some ways of dealing with conflict. | | | |
| I understand what peer groups mean and how peers can influence teenagers. | | | |

**The topic I most enjoyed in this chapter:** _____

**The topic I would like to learn more about:** _____

# Health and wellbeing

# 19

1. Explain what is meant by the term 'wellbeing'.

   ~~Wellbe~~ Wellbeing is the state of being comfortable, healthy and happy

2. How does a safe and nurturing home contribute to wellbeing?

   positive surroundings and as caring people looking after a child or teenager. Helps with dealing with when things go wrong, as a plan is put in place to deal with it!

3. State four guidelines for a healthy lifestyle.

   (a) Being immunised and vaccinated against diseases

   (b) regular exercise

   (c) enough rest and sleep

   (d) a balanced diet

4. Refer to Chapter 3 of your textbook and state four guidelines to make sure an active teenager has a balanced diet.

   (a) include protein and calcium for growth

   (b) active teenagers need lots of carbohydrates

   (c) ·inactive teenagers may become overweight on a high energy diet

   (d) a good supply of iron is important for teenage girls to prevent anaemia.

5. Explain what is meant by insomnia and suggest two possible causes.

   insomnia is not being able to sleep or sleeplessness. this can be caused by too much. caffeine – like in tea and coffee- or high levels of stress. High levels of stress can be a common cause of insomnia, as well as too much screen time.

6. Divide the following into lists of dos and don'ts to aid restful sleep.

| | Do | Don't | Reason |
|---|---|---|---|
| Use your tablet/phone in bed. | | ✓ | light makes it harder to sleep |
| Have a cup of coffee at bedtime. | | ✓ | caffeine makes it harder to sleep |
| Get some exercise during the day. | ✓ | | tires you out and is good for health. |
| Keep studying up until bedtime. | | ✓ | causes stress and possibly insomnia. |
| Take a warm bath during the evening. | ✓ | ~~✓~~ | relaxation |
| Make sure the bedroom is hot. | ~~✓~~ | ✓ | can make it harder to sleep |
| Keep the window closed day and night. | | ✓ | makes the room warm |
| Watch TV for a few hours before bedtime. | ~~✓~~ | ~~✓~~ ✓ | ~~makes you~~ ~~relaxation~~ can cause insomnia from screen time |
| Avoid eating late at night. | ✓ | | eating can wake you up. |

7. Give three benefits of using leisure time wisely.
   (a) reduces stress ✓
   (b) relieves boredom ✓
   (c) make more friends ✓

8. Suggest four benefits of being involved in team sports.
   (a) improves fitness level ✓
   (b) helps build confidence ✓
   (c) helps develop communication skills ✓
   (d) ~~improves health and~~ keeps muscles and joints flexible

9. Under the headings listed, suggest two leisure time activities for teenagers.

| | |
|---|---|
| **Sport** | ~~hockey~~ ~~tennis~~ hockey, tennis |
| **Indoor activities (other than sport)** | musical instrument, chess |
| **Outdoor activities (other than sport)** | walking, hiking |
| **Activities that benefit others** | volunteering, babysitting |

**10.** Explain how not having any interesting pastimes impacts on teenagers. List two possible effects.

(a) boredom, depression, loneliness

(b) lack of friends, less possibilities to make friends

**11.** Suggest two ways teenagers might benefit from being a member of a youth club.

(a) social aspect - making friends

(b) ~~physical~~ cultural aspect - day trips to parks, areas of interest

**12.** Identify two health problems associated with a lack of fitness.

(a) coronary heart disease ✓

(b) osteoperosis ✓

**13.** Outline two benefits of regular exercise.

(a) more efficient heart and lungs ✓

(b) can reduce high blood pressure ✓

**14.** What is aerobic exercise?

~~exerc~~ exercise that makes you breathless, so the lungs take in more oxygen. ✓

**15.** Refer to p. 45 of your textbook and list two other factors that help to reduce the risk of heart disease.

(a) reduce foods high in saturated/hydrogenated fats in diet

(b) ~~exer~~ exercise regularly ~~exercise~~

# Mental health

**1.** (a) What do you understand by mental health?

mental health is concerned with ~~the state~~ health and wellbeing of the mind

(b) Identify two characteristics of good mental health.

(i) being resilient

(ii) feeling reasonably content with life and having a positive attitude

**2.** Explain what you understand by the following terms:

(a) Attitudes the way you feel about life in general

(b) Under stress when someone experiences a lot of pressure or tension

3. Suggest two different causes of stress:

   **(a)** In adults

   (i) job loss

   (ii) relationship breakdowns

   **(b)** In adolescents

   (i) exams

   (ii) friendships

4. Give four symptoms associated with continuous stress.

   **(a)** anxiety

   **(b)** moodiness

   **(c)** aggression

   **(d)** overindulgence in food/alcohol

5. Suggest two ways to relieve stress caused by exams.

   **(a)** study - preparing well

   **(b)** being organised

6. Recommend two ways of ensuring safety while using the internet.

   **(a)** rules with parents/guardians

   **(b)** restrictions on websites used

# Personal hygiene

1. List four guidelines to follow to ensure personal hygiene.

   **(a)** wash regularly

   **(b)** brush teeth regularly

   **(c)** clean underwear/socks

   **(d)** wash hands frequently

2. What is plaque?

   saliva, bacteria and leftover food particles

   plaque is the build-up of ~~leftover food particles~~ on teeth

3. Explain why sweet foods contribute to tooth decay.

   high sugar foods produce the most acid which ~~the teeth~~ damages ~~the~~ decays the teeth

4. State four guidelines for caring for teeth.

   **(a)** brush teeth every day

   **(b)** limit sweet foods

   **(c)** visit dentist regularly

   **(d)** eat foods rich in calcium and vitamin D

5. Identify four oral hygiene products.

   **(a)** toothbrush

   **(b)** toothpaste

   **(c)** mouthwash

   **(d)** dental floss

6. What nutrients help to maintain healthy teeth?

   vitamin D and calcium

7. Recommend three guidelines to follow to ensure healthy skin.

   (a) avoid foods high in fat and sugar

   (b) drink plenty of water

   (c) keep skin clean

8. List two things you should avoid in order to have healthy skin.

   (a) overexposure to direct sunlight      (b) foods high in fat and sugar

9. Outline two ways of reducing the risk of skin cancer.

   (a) wear a sunhat or cap to protect head and face

   (b) use a high factor sun cream and reapply it regularly

10. Explain why each of the following is necessary to ensure a high standard of hygiene in the home.

    (a) Ventilation: to bring in fresh air

    (b) Good lighting: for eyesight and concentration

    (c) Heating: so the house does not get damp or too cold.

    (d) Careful waste disposal: prevents bacteria and germs spreading

# Responsible life choices

1. Identify three lifestyle choices that are damaging to health and wellbeing.

   (a) _____

   (b) _____

   (c) _____

2. Suggest two reasons why teenagers smoke.

   (a) _____

   (b) _____

3. Name three diseases linked with smoking.

   (a) _____  (b) _____  (c) _____

4. Why is it particularly dangerous for pregnant women to smoke?

   _____

5. State three ways in which the government tries to discourage young people from smoking.

   (a) _____

   (b) _____

   (c) _____

# Alcohol

1. Complete the following sentence.

   Alcohol contains the drug _____ which is _____.

2. State two risks for teenagers who drink alcohol.

   (a) _____

   (b) _____

3. Teenage drinking is on the increase in Ireland. Suggest two reasons for this.

   (a) _____

   (b) _____

4. State two immediate effects of alcohol on the body.

   (a) _____

   (b) _____

5. Identify four health problems that can develop from the long-term abuse of alcohol.

   (a) _____

   (b) _____

   (c) _____

   (d) _____

6. State two effects of alcohol abuse on:

   (a) The family of the abuser

       (i) _____

       (ii) _____

   (b) Society

       (i) _____

       (ii) _____

7. Name an organisation that helps people who have a problem with alcohol.

   _____

8. Write a brief note on each of the following organisations.

   (a) Al-Anon: _____

   _____

   (b) Alateen: _____

   _____

# Drugs

1. Explain the following terms.

   (a) Drug: _____

   (b) Drug abuse: _____

2. Give two examples of each of the following.

| Commonly used drugs | Controlled drugs | Illegal drugs |
|---|---|---|
| | | |
| | | |

3. Suggest two reasons why people abuse drugs.

   (a) _____

   _____

   (b) _____

   _____

4. Outline four effects of drug abuse on a person's health.

   (a) _____

   (b) _____

   (c) _____

   (d) _____

5. Outline two effects of drug abuse on society.

   (a) _____

   (b) _____

6. List two ways the family of a drug abuser is affected by his or her addiction.

   (a) _____

   _____

   (b) _____

   _____

7. What is meant by the term 'addiction'?

   _____

   _____

   _____

# Over to you 👉

1. Are the following statements true or false?

| Statement | True | False |
|---|:---:|:---:|
| One in every 10 smokers will die of a tobacco-related illness. | ○ | ○ |
| Children of smokers do not suffer any ill effects as a result of their parents smoking. | ○ | ○ |
| Approximately 5,000 people die in Ireland each year from smoking-related illnesses. | ○ | ○ |
| Ethyl alcohol is an addictive drug. | ○ | ○ |
| Drinking alcohol increases a person's powers of judgement. | ○ | ○ |
| Prolonged abuse of alcohol may lead to heart disease. | ○ | ○ |
| An alcoholic can be cured. | ○ | ○ |
| Caffeine is a legal drug. | ○ | ○ |
| Sleeping pills can be bought over the counter. | ○ | ○ |
| Drug abusers might die from AIDS. | ○ | ○ |
| Drugs can only be injected. | ○ | ○ |
| Al-Anon is an organisation that helps drug abusers. | ○ | ○ |

2. Make a poster of suggestions for a healthy lifestyle and display it in school.

3. Examine the following case study and answer the questions that follow.

# Case study

Holly is a pretty girl who is careless about her appearance. She seldom has a bath or a shower. She has a favourite pair of runners that she wears constantly. Her hair tends to be very greasy because it is long and difficult to dry. She only washes it once a week. Her fringe hides the spots on her forehead. She has nice nails that she keeps long and painted, but she finds it hard to keep them clean. In the evenings when doing her homework, she absentmindedly touches her face. She hates exercise and avoids PE when she can. Her favourite pastime is watching TV while eating crisps and sweets, and as a result Holly has put on a lot of weight. Recently she heard a girl in her class calling her a slob and she was very hurt by the remark.

(a) Suggest ways Holly can change her lifestyle and improve her appearance.

(b) Make a list and cost the items you feel are necessary in order to maintain a high standard of personal hygiene.

# Learning checklist

| | | | |
|---|:-:|:-:|:-:|
| **Red: I don't know this.** Orange**: I need to study this again.** Green**: Good to go!** | ● | ● | ● |
| I can appreciate the value of being healthy and physically active. | | | |
| I can understand the importance of good mental health in managing the demands of daily life. | | | |
| I can explain what is meant by attitudes and I can give examples. | | | |
| I can list some causes of stress and I know some ways of relieving stress. | | | |
| I am aware of the importance of personal hygiene to health and wellbeing. | | | |
| I can explain how to care for teeth in order to keep them healthy. | | | |
| I know how to ensure that I have healthy skin. | | | |
| I appreciate the seriousness of skin cancer and I know how to reduce the risk of skin cancer. | | | |
| I am aware of the importance of household hygiene to health and wellbeing. | | | |
| I can suggest some reasons why people start to smoke. | | | |
| I can list the effects of alcohol abuse on the family and society. | | | |
| I can identify where help is available for people affected by alcohol abuse or drug abuse. | | | |
| I can list the effects of drug abuse. | | | |
| I can discuss the requirements of a safe and nurturing home. | | | |

**The topic I most enjoyed in this chapter:** _____

**The topic I would like to learn more about:** _____

# 20 The consumer

## Consumers

1. Define the following terms.

   (a) Consumer: _____

   (b) Needs: _____

   (c) Wants: _____

   (d) Priorities: _____

2. Indicate in the table below whether you think each of the following are needs or wants for a family on a low budget:

   Rent                  Jewellery              Magazines              Health insurance

   Cinema                School uniforms        Electricity            Designer fashions

   Food                  Foreign holiday

   | Needs | Wants |
   |-------|-------|
   |       |       |
   |       |       |
   |       |       |
   |       |       |
   |       |       |

3. Outline two factors that influence needs.

   (a) _____

   (b) _____

4. Suggest what might be the priorities of each of the following people:

   (a) A very wealthy teenager living in New York

   _____

   (b) A seven-year-old boy working as a cotton picker in India

   _____

   (c) A 20-year-old wheelchair user who has just finished at university and is living in Dublin

   _____

   (d) An elderly woman living in a very rough housing estate in London

   _____

**5.** Examine the case study below.

## Case study

Maly is an eight-year-old girl living in Cambodia. Her father died three years ago. She works with her mother and sister in a brick factory. They work from 6 a.m. to 6 p.m. in intense heat. Pay is poor. Maly is often exhausted and never has enough to eat. Her mother is getting older and weaker and Maly knows she has no choice but to keep working.

(a) What rights do you think Maly has?

_____

(b) What responsibilities does she have?

_____

(c) What are her priorities?

_____

(d) What rights would she have as an eight-year-old-child if she were living in Ireland?

_____

**6.** Complete the following diagram.

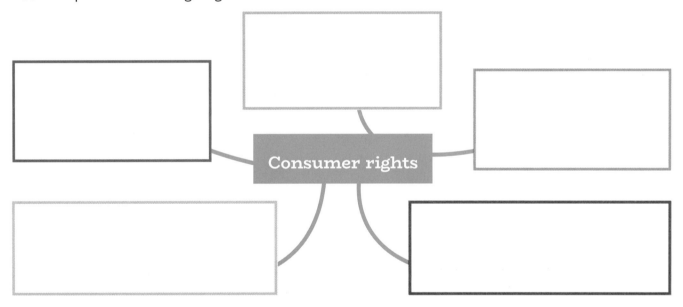

Consumer rights

**7.** Goods on sale must be of merchantable quality. Explain what is meant by merchantable quality.

_____

_____

**8. (a)** What is meant by the term 'redress'?

_____

**(b)** Identify two forms of redress.

(i) _____

(ii) _____

9. State two consumer responsibilities.

    (a) _____

    (b) _____

10. (a) What is a resource?

    _____

    (b) Name two consumer resources.

        (i) _____  (ii) _____

# Consumer information

1. Suggest two reasons why consumers need to be informed.

    (a) _____

    (b) _____

2. Name three sources of consumer information and state one advantage and one disadvantage of each source.

| Source | Advantage | Disadvantage |
|--------|-----------|--------------|
|        |           |              |
|        |           |              |
|        |           |              |

3. Indicate whether each of the following is true or false.

| Statement | True | False |
|-----------|------|-------|
| All consumers have a right to product safety. | ○ | ○ |
| A consumer is a person who sells goods and services. | ○ | ○ |
| A consumer has a right to redress when an item is faulty. | ○ | ○ |

# Consumer laws

1. Name two laws that protect the consumer.

    (a) _____

    (b) _____

2. Complete the following sentences using the words given below:

| consumer | advertising | price |
|---|---|---|
| Protection | services | claims |

The Consumer _____ Act protects the _____ against false or misleading

_____ about goods and _____. False claims made in _____ and

misleading information regarding _____ .

3. Give two examples of claims in each case:

| Goods claims | Services claims |
|---|---|
|  |  |
|  |  |

4. Fill in the blanks from the words given below:

| Services | merchantable |
|---|---|
| purpose | Goods |
| described | sample |
| 1980 | |

The Sale of _____ and Supply of _____ Act of _____ lays down

the following conditions:

(a) Goods should be of _____ quality.

(b) Goods should be fit for their _____.

(c) Goods must be as _____.

(d) Goods must conform to any _____.

5. Explain what is meant by:

(a) As described _____

_____

(b) Conform to sample _____

_____

6. Choose the correct word from the following list to complete (a) and (b) below.

| redress | guarantee | credit note |
|---|---|---|

(a) A consumer has a right to _____ if goods are faulty.

(b) A _____ is an undertaking that goods will be satisfactory for a stated length of time.

7. Under the Sale of Goods and Supply of Services Act, all warranties (written guarantees) must meet certain conditions.

## GUARANTEE (Burton washing machine)

(These statements do not affect a Consumer's statutory rights.)

Burton appliances carry a one-year parts and labour guarantee plus free replacement parts for the first 10 years, provided that they are fitted by our own service engineers. This product is sold subject to the understanding that should any defect in manufacture or material appear within one year from the date of consumer sale, the defect will be rectified without charge provided:

1. The product is registered with us or reasonable evidence is supplied (e.g. purchase receipt) that the product was purchased not more than 12 months prior to the date of the claim.

2. The defect is not due to accidental damage (whether in transit or otherwise), misuse, neglect, or inexpert repair.

Should service be required please apply to the retailer from whom the product was purchased or contact our Consumer Help Line at 1880 234 5111.

Indicate (tick) whether the above warranty for a washing machine meets the following conditions:

| | Yes | No |
|---|---|---|
| Is clear and legible | ◯ | ◯ |
| Refers to specific goods | ◯ | ◯ |
| States the name of the company offering the guarantee and against which claims should be made | ◯ | ◯ |
| Has the period of the guarantee (from the date of purchase) clearly stated | ◯ | ◯ |
| Describes the procedure for making claims | ◯ | ◯ |
| States what the manufacturer undertakes to do in relation to unsatisfactory goods | ◯ | ◯ |
| States what costs the buyer must meet if goods become faulty under guarantee | ◯ | ◯ |

8. State two rights that consumers have when availing of services.

(a) _____

(b) _____

**9.** Identify two different forms of redress that apply to goods and services.

| Goods | Services |
|---|---|
|  |  |
|  |  |

**10.** List two types of services available to people in the home and two available outside the home.

| In the home | Outside the home |
|---|---|
|  |  |
|  |  |

**11.** State two features of good quality service you would expect:

    **(a)** In a hotel

        **(i)** _____

       **(ii)** _____

    **(b)** From a window cleaner

        **(i)** _____

       **(ii)** _____

**12.** Explain why consumer protection is necessary.

_____

_____

_____

_____

**13.** Indicate whether each of the following is true or false.

| Statement | True | False |
|---|---|---|
| A partial refund means getting all your money back. | ◯ | ◯ |
| Merchantable quality means goods must be of a reasonably good standard. | ◯ | ◯ |
| Redress means compensation for faulty goods. | ◯ | ◯ |
| A credit note may be given for faulty goods. | ◯ | ◯ |
| A guarantee must always be given with goods. | ◯ | ◯ |
| Services are not covered by consumer law. | ◯ | ◯ |

# Consumer complaints

1. Outline one situation in which:

(a) The consumer may be entitled to a full refund. _____

_____

(b) The consumer is not entitled to a full refund. _____

_____

(c) The consumer complaint is unjustified. _____

_____

2. Define the following terms.

(a) Receipt: _____

(b) Credit note: _____

3. State three pieces of information found on a receipt.

(a) _____

(b) _____

(c) _____

4. Explain one benefit to the consumer of keeping a receipt.

_____

_____

5. Name one statutory and one non-statutory consumer protection agency and state two functions of each agency.

| | Statutory agency | Non-statutory agency |
|---|---|---|
| Name | | |
| Functions | | |
| | | |

6. List four pieces of information that should be included in a letter of complaint.

(a) _____

(b) _____

(c) _____

(d) _____

# Quality control

1. State three characteristics of good quality in each case.

| Products | Goods |
| --- | --- |
|  |  |
|  |  |
|  |  |

2. Illustrate one quality mark and one safety symbol. Indicate where each might be found.

_____

_____

## Over to you

1. Examine the following case study and answer the questions that follow.

### Case study

Brian is a 13-year-old student. He gets up at 7:30 a.m. every morning and has breakfast before catching the bus to school. He had classes all day and has lunch in the school canteen with some friends. After school he has football training at the local pitch. Then he usually goes to the public library to do some homework and project research. His mother picks him up at the library.

On Fridays, they go to the shopping centre. Brian usually helps his mother with the grocery shopping or may get a haircut or buy things he needs for project work such as graph paper. When they get home they have dinner, then Brian may try to finish his homework because he has a match most Saturdays. Afterwards he plays some computer games and watches TV.

   (a) List some goods that Brian and his mother bought.

   (b) List some services that Brian used during the day.

2. Role-play: In groups act out the following scenarios.

   (a) A teenager returns a faulty phone to a store. Role-play the scene in the store where:

      (i) He gets an unhelpful reaction    (ii) The reaction is favourable

   (b) A washing machine that was just serviced leaks and floods the utility room. Role-play the phone call to the service supplier:

      (i) Where the reaction is unhelpful    (ii) Where the complaint is dealt with in a polite and helpful manner

3. Watch and listen carefully to five TV advertisements, note the claims made by the suppliers of the goods and services in these advertisements, then fill out the table below.

| Product/service advertised | Claim made |
|---|---|
| 1. | |
| 2. | |
| 3. | |
| 4. | |
| 5. | |

4. Draw each of the quality and safety symbols and display in the classroom.

# Learning checklist

| Red: **I don't know this.** Orange: **I need to study this again.** Green: **Good to go!** | ● | ● | ● |
|---|---|---|---|
| I can define the terms 'consumer', 'goods', 'services', 'needs' and 'wants' and I can give examples of each. | | | |
| I can debate the rights and responsibilities of consumers. | | | |
| I can apply the skills needed to be a discerning consumer. | | | |
| I understand why consumers need to be informed and I can evaluate different sources of consumer information. | | | |
| I can name two laws that protect the consumer and I can outline what is covered in these laws. | | | |
| I understand what is meant by the terms 'redress' and 'guarantee'. | | | |
| I can explain why consumer protection is necessary. | | | |
| I appreciate when consumer complaints are justified and when they are not. | | | |
| I can name and state the function of two statutory and two non-statutory consumer agencies. | | | |
| I can outline the procedure involved when making a complaint. | | | |
| I understand what is meant by good quality and quality control. | | | |
| I can demonstrate effective communication when composing a letter or email of complaint. | | | |
| I can list characteristics of good quality in products and services. | | | |
| I recognise the different quality and safety symbols and know where each symbol might be found. | | | |
| **The topic I most enjoyed in this chapter:** _____ | | | |
| **The topic I would like to learn more about:** _____ | | | |

# Decision-making

1. State three reasons why it is important to make informed decisions.

   (a) _____

   (b) _____

   (c) _____

2. Rewrite the following decision-making steps in the correct order:

   * Make a decision
   * Consider alternatives and consequences of each
   * Evaluate results
   * Put decision into action
   * Collect information
   * Identify problem

   (a) _____

   (b) _____

   (c) _____

   (d) _____

   (e) _____

   (f) _____

3. Identify four areas of management that are involved in running a home.

   (a) _____

   (b) _____

   (c) _____

   (d) _____

4. Identify the steps involved in a management system.

   (a) _____

   (b) _____

   (c) _____

   (d) _____

   (e) _____

5. List six resources that would be used while cleaning the home.

   (a) _____  (b) _____  (c) _____

   (d) _____  (e) _____  (f) _____

6. List four cleaning agents. Give a use for each agent.

| Cleaning agent | Use |
|---|---|
|  |  |
|  |  |
|  |  |
|  |  |

7. Outline four factors to consider when choosing cleaning agents.

(a) _____

(b) _____

(c) _____

(d) _____

8. State two guidelines to follow when using cleaning agents.

(a) _____

_____

(b) _____

_____

9. Suggest two guidelines to ensure safety when storing cleaning agents.

(a) _____

(b) _____

10. (a) What is meant by the term 'ergonomics'? _____

_____

(b) State two examples of where ergonomics applies in home management.

(i) _____

(ii) _____

11. Give the order of work to follow when cleaning a room.

(a) _____

(b) _____

(c) _____

(d) _____

(e) _____

(f) _____

**12. (a)** Examine the case study below and answer the question that follows.

## Case study

Jack sets about cleaning the downstairs windows. He goes to the garage to collect a bucket. He fills the bucket at the kitchen sink. He then returns to the garage to get a cloth. He collects the bucket from the sink, decides to start at the front and walks through the house carrying the bucket. He trips and spills some water outside the house but fills it up with the tap on the outside of the house. He then travels back through the house to the garage to get a stool to stand on. Jack washes the first window on the outside and has to stretch to reach the top. He then walks through the house again to get newspaper to polish the window. On returning with the newspaper, Jack sees that the window has dried and is streaky – he had better wash it again! It looks like this chore is going to take a long time.

**(b)** Give Jack some tips on how to save time and energy.

_____

_____

_____

_____

_____

**13.** Explain what is meant by a resource.

_____

**14.** Insert the following resources into the correct column in the table.

| Hospital | Books | Skills |
|---|---|---|
| Time | Energy | Libraries |
| Food | Schools | Cleaning agents |

| Human resources | Commodities | Community resources |
|---|---|---|
|  |  |  |
|  |  |  |
|  |  |  |

**15.** Suggest three resources that might be used for each of the following.

**(a)** Playing a football match: _____

_____

**(b)** Writing an essay: _____

_____

**(c)** Baking a cake: _____

_____

(d) Making a cushion cover: _____

_____

(e) Planning a grocery shopping list: _____

_____

(f) Going on a school trip: _____

_____

16. Indicate whether the following are internal or external factors that influence your choice of goods and services.

| | Internal factors | External factors |
|---|---|---|
| Current fashion trends | | |
| Your friends | | |
| Your preferences | | |
| Cost | | |
| Your needs | | |
| Advertising | | |

17. What two factors do you think most influence teenagers when buying clothes?

(a) _____

(b) _____

18. Complete the following steps in a budgeting management system.

(a) Set a _____     (b) Identify _____     (c) Make a _____

(d) Act on _____     (e) Evaluate _____

19. Explain the following terms.

(a) Money management: _____

(b) A budget: _____

(c) Gross income: _____

20. Differentiate between voluntary and statutory deductions. Give an example in each case.

| | Explanation | Example |
|---|---|---|
| Voluntary deduction | | |
| Statutory deduction | | |

**21.** Explain each of the following statutory deductions and indicate for what the money is used.

| | Explanation | Used for |
|---|---|---|
| PAYE | | |
| PRSI | | |

**22.** Distinguish between gross and net income. _____
_____

**23.** Explain the following terms.

(a) Tax credits: _____
_____

(b) Take-home pay: _____
_____

**24.** Examine the case study below.

## Case study

Alan has just started work in a technology firm. He is paid €900 every fortnight. Most evenings he goes for a few pints to the local with a group from the office. On payday, he goes greyhound racing with two friends. He loves the track and has found a brilliant app that allows him to bet online. He eats out or gets takeaways most evenings and buys his lunch and several cups of coffee throughout the day. He likes his job and is well paid but he wonders why he is broke all the time!

(a) What advice would you give to Alan to help him manage his money better?

_____

_____

_____

(b) Design a weekly budget for Alan.

| Budget | % income | € |
|---|---|---|
| | | |
| | | |
| | | |
| | | |

25. (a) Explain the term 'impulse buying'. _____

_____

(b) Give an example of when impulse buying might be a good idea.

_____

26. What factors influence where a person chooses to save?

(a) _____

(b) _____

27. Suggest two advantages for young workers of saving regularly.

(a) _____

(b) _____

28. What are the advantages of having a home filing system?

_____

29. Differentiate between a paper-based and paperless filing systems.

_____

_____

# Over to you

1. (a) Make a list of all the decisions you have made already today.

(b) Can you suggest any more difficult decisions you may have to make in the near future?

2. Select three cleaning agents that can be used to clean kitchen surfaces. Compare them under the following headings:

| | Cleaning agent 1 | Cleaning agent 2 | Cleaning agent 3 |
|---|---|---|---|
| Cost | | | |
| Packaging (e.g. plastic or biodegradable) | | | |
| Effect on the environment or ozone layer | | | |
| Variety of uses | | | |
| Effectiveness | | | |
| Safety – is it harmful? | | | |
| Labelling – clear instructions, warnings | | | |

3. Plan a budget for a young worker with a net income of €320 a week who is living independently. Illustrate the budget on a bar or pie chart.

# Learning checklist

| | | | |
|---|:-:|:-:|:-:|
| **Red: I don't know this.** Orange: **I need to study this again.** Green: **Good to go!** | ⬤ | ⬤ | ⬤ |
| I understand the importance of making informed and responsible decisions in everyday life. | | | |
| I can apply the decision-making process when choosing a product or service. | | | |
| I can identify areas of management within the home. | | | |
| I can work with others to apply a management system. | | | |
| I can state points to consider when buying and using cleaning agents. | | | |
| I understand what is meant by ergonomics and I can devise a work plan for cleaning. | | | |
| I can identify the resources available to us. | | | |
| I can state some factors that influence our decisions when choosing goods and services. | | | |
| I understand what is meant by money management. | | | |
| I can apply financial literacy skills in the preparation of a budget. | | | |
| I can appreciate the advantages of budgeting. | | | |
| I can list the savings institutions and the advantages of saving. | | | |
| I understand the factors to consider when choosing a place to save. | | | |
| I understand the necessity for a home filing system and can list some examples. | | | |

**The topic I most enjoyed in this chapter:** _____

**The topic I would like to learn more about:** _____

# 22 Design in the home

1. Complete the following sentences.

   Shelter is a basic _____. Houses provide us with_____. They protect us

   from _____.

2. Match the people listed in column A with suitable accommodation in column B:

   | A | B |
   |---|---|
   | A university student | Nursing home |
   | A wheelchair user | Small apartment |
   | A young couple | Bungalow |
   | A family with young children | Student accommodation |
   | An elderly woman with health problems | Four-bedroom semi-detached house with garden |

3. State four factors that influence the choice of housing.

   (a) _____

   (b) _____

   (c) _____

   (d) _____

4. Give one example of energy efficiency in housing.

   _____

   _____

5. Define the following terms.

   (a) Community: _____

   (b) Amenities: _____

6. Give two examples each of amenities, statutory services and voluntary services in your community.

   | Amenities | Statutory services | Voluntary services |
   |---|---|---|
   | | | |
   | | | |

**7.** Suggest three reasons why people become homeless.

(a) _____

(b) _____

(c) _____

**8.** Complete the following sentences:

A design is a _____ or _____ for the production of something such as

a_____ or _____. A good design is a_____, f_____,

d_____, s_____ and e_____ f_____.

**9.** Fill in the design features in the diagram below.

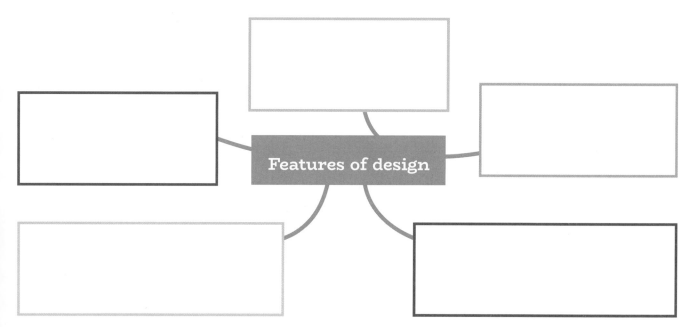

**10.** Colour in the colour wheel and indicate whether each colour is a primary or a secondary colour.

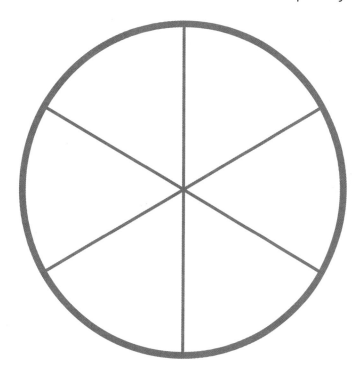

**11. (a)** How is a tertiary colour produced?

_____

_____

**(b)** Give an example of a tertiary colour. _____

**12.** Match the terms in column A with a colour in column B.

| A | B |
|---|---|
| Secondary colour | Turquoise |
| Neutral colour | Pastels |
| Primary colour | Tint |
| Tertiary colour | Blue |
| Pale shades of colour | Orange |
| Adding white to a colour | White |

**13.** Describe the effect of each of the following types of colours, giving an example of each:

| Colour | Effect | Examples |
|---|---|---|
| Warm colours | | |
| Cool colours | | |
| Neutrals | | |
| Pastels | | |

**14.** Differentiate between the following colour terms.

**(a)** Tint: _____

**(b)** Shade: _____

**15. (a)** Texture refers to _____.

**(b)** Suggest four examples of each texture:

| Rough textures | Smooth textures |
|---|---|
| | |
| | |
| | |
| | |

**16.** Complete the following table about lines.

| Lines | Effect | Diagram |
|---|---|---|
| **Diagonal lines** | | |
| **Horizontal lines** | | |

**17. (a)** Shape refers to _____ .

**(b)** Draw four basic shapes.

| | | | |
|---|---|---|---|
| | | | |

**18.** What is the effect of using too much pattern in a room?

_____

_____

# Design principles

**1.** Match the design principle from column A with a suitable definition from column B.

| A | B |
|---|---|
| Rhythm | Draws attention to a particular feature. |
| Balance | Repeated use of a pattern or colour. |
| Emphasis | Furniture pieces relate to one another and to the size of the room. |
| Proportion | All parts of the design work well together. |

2. Identify four characteristics of a well-planned room.

(a) _____

(b) _____

(c) _____

(d) _____

3. Explain how aspect affects room planning.

_____

_____

4. Why is it important to consider traffic flow when planning a room?

_____

_____

5. (a) Apply the design principles and room planning guidelines to complete the room plan for a teenager's room by drawing the following to scale in the room: bed, locker, desk and chair, bookcase, chest of drawers or dressing table and wardrobe.

(b) Suggest two ways to personalise the room or to reflect the teenager's hobbies.

(i) _____

(ii) _____

6. Give one reason why each of the following might not be suitable for a bedroom.

(a) Ceramic floor tiles: _____

(b) Fluorescent lighting: _____

(c) Gas heater: _____

7. Suggest four soft furnishings suitable for (a) a sitting room and (b) a child's bedroom.

   (a) (i) _____ (ii) _____

       (iii) _____ (iv) _____

   (b) (i) _____ (ii) _____

       (iii) _____ (iv) _____

8. Kitchens need to be well planned. State four factors that must be considered when planning a kitchen.

   (a) _____ (b) _____

   (c) _____ (d) _____

9. Outline the sequence that should be followed when preparing food.

   | | | | |
   |---|---|---|---|
   | | | | |

10. Suggest two reasons why kitchen sinks are often placed under a window.

    (a) _____ (b) _____

11. (a) Design a kitchen room plan and include the work sequence and work triangle.

    (b) What is the benefit of using a work triangle in kitchen design?

    _____

    _____

**12.** Suggest one suitable and one unsuitable floor covering for a kitchen and give a reason in each case.

| | Suitable | Unsuitable |
|---|---|---|
| | | |
| **Reason** | | |

# Over to you ☞

**1.** Find the features and principles of design in the word search.

| BALANCE | LINE | RHYTHM |
|---|---|---|
| COLOUR | PATTERN | SHAPE |
| EMPHASIS | PROPORTION | TEXTURE |

| E | K | P | G | Y | A | R | N | N | G | F | R | I | T | Y |
|---|---|---|---|---|---|---|---|---|---|---|---|---|---|---|
| R | X | R | N | R | U | B | I | R | M | M | Q | W | J | U |
| U | K | O | Q | O | V | C | M | T | E | T | U | F | K | O |
| T | L | P | L | L | I | B | H | A | L | T | Q | C | I | R |
| X | N | O | Y | M | E | I | U | J | R | Y | T | U | A | C |
| E | C | R | Q | B | O | S | O | F | E | V | A | A | I | V |
| T | N | T | R | H | Y | T | H | M | M | J | Q | M | P | Q |
| Y | Y | I | P | L | M | O | P | A | G | D | S | I | U | H |
| D | X | O | Y | K | M | H | A | M | P | O | V | O | J | L |
| O | J | N | B | K | A | X | X | W | A | E | M | L | U | S |
| D | J | P | W | S | E | C | N | A | L | A | B | G | R | A |
| V | Z | X | I | G | M | Z | E | V | I | Y | H | M | N | L |
| L | I | S | P | R | U | N | K | A | N | I | H | F | N | K |
| O | A | P | A | O | Z | J | A | P | E | V | D | Z | G | S |
| A | U | P | G | X | E | W | P | Q | S | E | F | P | T | Q |

**2.** Look through magazines or research online to find examples of the following design principles: balance, emphasis, proportion, rhythm and keep them in your folder.

**3.** Using pictures from magazines, newspapers or online, find examples of the each of the following used in interior design. Make a collage of the pictures and display it in the classroom.

**(a)** Warm colours     **(b)** Cool colours     **(c)** Neutral colours

**(d)** Pastel colours     **(e)** Large patterns     **(f)** Small patterns

**(g)** Obvious patterns     **(h)** Inconspicuous patterns

# Learning checklist

| Red: **I don't know this.** Orange: **I need to study this again.** Green: **Good to go!** | ● | ● | ● |
|---|---|---|---|
| I can distinguish between a house and a home. | | | |
| I can list some factors that influence the choice of housing. | | | |
| I know what is meant by community services and amenities and I can give examples of both. | | | |
| I can outline the features and principles of design. | | | |
| I can apply the design principles and guidelines to the design of a living space in a family home. | | | |
| I can list the points to consider when planning a room and the features of a well-planned room. | | | |
| I can design and draw room plans and I can outline the order of work when decorating a room. | | | |
| I can imagine what a well-planned room would look like. | | | |
| I appreciate how ergonomics is used in kitchen planning. | | | |
| I understand the importance of the work sequence and work triangle when planning a kitchen. | | | |

**The topic I most enjoyed in this chapter:** _____

**The topic I would like to learn more about:** _____

# 23 Technology in the home

## Technology

1. (a) Define technology.

   _____

   (b) Identify three ways in which you use technology in day-to-day life.

   (i) _____

   (ii) _____

   (iii) _____

2. Complete the table on the advantages of technology in the following areas:

| | Advantage 1 | Advantage 2 |
|---|---|---|
| Food preparation | | |
| Household materials | | |
| Cleaning/maintenance | | |

3. Name four cordless appliances.

   (a) _____   (b) _____

   (c) _____   (d) _____

4. Name two easy-to-clean surfaces used for household resources.

   (a) _____   (b) _____

5. List four pieces of technology commonly used for entertainment.

   (a) _____   (b) _____

   (c) _____   (d) _____

6. State four uses of computers in the home.

   (a) _____

   (b) _____

   (c) _____

   (d) _____

**7.** Classify electrical equipment into three groups, giving two examples in each group.

| Electrical equipment | Examples |
| --- | --- |
|  |  |
|  |  |
|  |  |

**8.** Indicate whether each of the following electrical appliances has a heating element or a motor.

| Appliance | Heating element | Motor |
| --- | --- | --- |
| Toaster | ◯ | ◯ |
| Food mixer | ◯ | ◯ |
| Kettle | ◯ | ◯ |
| Carving knife | ◯ | ◯ |
| Deep-fat fryer | ◯ | ◯ |
| Hair dryer | ◯ | ◯ |
| Hair straightener | ◯ | ◯ |

**9.** Outline four factors to consider when buying a washing machine.

(a) _____    (b) _____

(c) _____    (d) _____

**10.** Suggest four guidelines to follow to ensure safety when using electrical appliances.

(a) _____    (b) _____

(c) _____    (d) _____

# Refrigerators

**1.** Sketch a diagram of a refrigerator. Include the following labels:

  ✳ Metal cabinet
  ✳ Icebox
  ✳ Shelves
  ✳ Salad drawer
  ✳ Light

**2. (a)** What is the recommended temperature for a fridge?_____

**(b)** How is the temperature controlled? _____

**3.** State four reasons why we use refrigerators.

**(a)** _____     **(b)** _____

**(c)** _____     **(d)** _____

**4.** Name three foods commonly stored in the refrigerator and state in which area of the fridge it should be stored. Explain why.

| Food | Fridge position | Reason |
|---|---|---|
|  |  |  |
|  |  |  |
|  |  |  |

**5.** In relation to the refrigerator, explain why it is important to:

**(a)** Position the refrigerator away from a heat source. _____

_____

**(b)** Cool food before putting it in the fridge. _____

_____

**(c)** Check the contents daily. _____

_____

**(d)** Open the door as little as possible. _____

_____

**6.** Give four guidelines on cleaning a refrigerator.

**(a)** _____     **(b)** _____

**(c)** _____     **(d)** _____

**7. (a)** Complete the following sentence:

Raw food is stored _____ cooked food in the refrigerator in order to prevent

_____ _____.

**(b)** What is meant by defrosting? _____

**(c)** Why is bread soda used to clean a fridge? _____

**8.** List three modern features of fridges.

**(a)** _____

**(b)** _____

**(c)** _____

**9.** Outline four points that should be considered when choosing a household refrigerator.

(a) _____

(b) _____

(c) _____

(d) _____

**10.** Complete the following sentences:

The star rating relates to the temperature of the _____ of the fridge. It indicates how

long frozen food can be _____ in the icebox.

**11.** Fill in the following table on the star rating of fridge-freezers:

| | |
|---|---|
| * One star | |
| | Stores frozen food for one month |
| *** Three star | |
| | Can freeze fresh food |

**12.** What does WEEE mean? _____

**13.** Explain how to safely dispose of a fridge using WEEE. _____

_____

**14.** Indicate whether the following statements are true or false:

| Statement | True | False |
|---|:---:|:---:|
| Technology has made home maintenance easier. | ○ | ○ |
| Kettles, irons and toasters may be cordless. | ○ | ○ |
| A washing machine has a heating element. | ○ | ○ |
| D is a good rating on an energy appliance. | ○ | ○ |
| Three stars means the temperature of the icebox is –12°C. | ○ | ○ |
| All freezers have a four-star marking. | ○ | ○ |

# Over to you

**1.** Research and find out the recommended temperatures for (a) a living room (b) a kitchen (c) a bedroom and (d) a freezer.

(a) _____     (b) _____

(c) _____     (d) _____

2. Working in groups, choose one piece of technology used in food preparation. Do a project on the appliance and present your findings under the headings: Brands; Prices; Energy efficiency. Include sketches, pictures or photographs of the appliance. Present your findings to the class.

3. Make a wall chart of a fridge interior and indicate where you would store each of the following: (a) peppers (b) cucumber (c) milk (d) leftover cooked chicken (e) butter (f) fresh lamb chops.

   Display the wall chart over the refrigerator in the Home Economics room.

4. (a) Carry out a survey within the class to find out how much time is spent daily:
   * Using technology
   * Being active
   * Reading

   (b) Draw a bar chart to represent your findings.

# Learning checklist

| Red: **I don't know this.** Orange: **I need to study this again.** Green: **Good to go!** | | | |
|---|---|---|---|
| I understand how technology influences management of resources in the home. | | | |
| I can classify electrical equipment used in the home. | | | |
| I can apply my knowledge when buying electrical equipment. | | | |
| I can list the advantages of using a fridge. | | | |
| I know how to care for and clean a fridge. | | | |
| I understand the star rating of fridges. | | | |
| I recognise the need to dispose of fridges safely. | | | |
| I appreciate the influence of technology on the management of personal and family resources. | | | |

**The topic I most enjoyed in this chapter:** _____

**The topic I would like to learn more about:** _____

# Sustainable and responsible living

1. Complete the following sentence.

   Sustainable living aims to reduce our _____ _____ and to conserve the

   earth's _____ _____ for future _____.

2. Name two possible causes of pollution in the table below.

| Types of pollution | Two possible causes of pollution |
| --- | --- |
| Air pollution | |
| Water pollution | |
| Noise pollution | |

3. Indicate whether the following statements are true or false.

| Statement | True | False |
| --- | --- | --- |
| Disposable products contribute to waste problems. | ○ | ○ |
| Acid rain is polluted rainfall. | ○ | ○ |
| The ozone layer harms the earth. | ○ | ○ |
| Water is a natural resource. | ○ | ○ |

4. Distinguish between organic and inorganic waste.

   _____

   _____

   _____

5. Place the following waste under the correct headings in the table below.

   Glass      Food      Plastic

   Paper      Metal      Grass cuttings

| Organic waste | Inorganic waste |
| --- | --- |
| | |
| | |
| | |

**6.** Complete the diagram of the EU waste hierarchy.

_____

_____

_____

_____

_____

_____

Most sustainable

Least sustainable

**7.** Suggest three ways that you could help reduce waste.

(a) _____

(b) _____

(c) _____

**8.** (a) What is meant by recycling? _____

(b) State two advantages of recycling for the environment.

(i) _____

(ii) _____

(c) Draw the recycling symbol.

**9.** How could the following be recycled?

(a) Old clothes: _____

(b) Grass cuttings: _____

(c) Glass jars: _____

(d) Newspapers: _____

**10.** List four types of waste that are suitable for composting.

(a) _____   (b) _____

(c) _____   (d) _____

**11.** Place the waste in the correct bin.

| Plastic bottles | Stale bread | Ashes | Tea bags |
| Vegetable peelings | Cereal box | Bean cans | Paper |
| Nappies | | | |

_____   _____   _____

_____   _____   _____

_____   _____   _____

**12.** See p. 270 of your textbook and answer the following:

(a) WEEE = _____ _____ and _____ _____

(b) Name three pieces of equipment that can be recycled under this scheme.

(i) _____   (ii) _____   (iii) _____

(c) Explain the value to the consumer of WEEE.

_____

_____

_____

**13.** How do the following benefit the consumer?

(a) Building Energy Rating (BER) _____

_____

_____

(b) Compact fluorescent lights (CFLs) _____

_____

**14.** State four ways of conserving energy when using a central heating system.

(a) _____   (b) _____

(c) _____   (d) _____

**15. (a)** The average daily water usage is _____ per person.

    **(b)** The main uses of water include:

        **(i)** _____

        **(ii)** _____

        **(iii)** _____

**16.** Suggest four ways of conserving hot water.

    **(a)** _____      **(b)** _____

    **(c)** _____      **(d)** _____

**17.** Are the following statements true or false?

| Statement | True | False |
|---|---|---|
| It is more energy efficient to take a bath instead of a shower. | ○ | ○ |
| Dishwashers should be full before use. | ○ | ○ |
| A timer controls the temperature of a heating system. | ○ | ○ |
| Good insulation conserves heat. | ○ | ○ |

**18.** List two ways of shopping in an environmentally friendly way.

    **(a)** _____      **(b)** _____

**19.** State three ways to be environmentally aware when heating the home.

    **(a)** _____    **(b)** _____    **(c)** _____

**20.** Give one reason for each of the following.

    **(a)** Planting trees: _____

    **(b)** Insulating the home: _____

    _____

    **(c)** Avoiding disposable products: _____

    **(d)** Using smokeless fuels: _____

**21.** Identify four materials that can be recycled.

    **(a)** _____      **(b)** _____

    **(c)** _____      **(d)** _____

**22.** Suggest two reasons why consumers should protect their environment.

    **(a)** _____      **(b)** _____

**23.** Name one agency or programme concerned with the environment.

    _____

# Over to you 👉

1. Design and laminate small posters to put above light switches and electrical sockets to remind people to switch them off when not in use. Display these reminders in every classroom throughout the school.

2. Draw up a set of guidelines to help reduce food waste during practical cookery classes. Display these guidelines on a poster in the Home Economics room.

3. Read and discuss the following paragraph.

   In Brazil over 50,000 children earn a living by scavenging through the city rubbish dumps. They are searching for food and recyclable goods. They are paid per bag load of collected paper, glass or plastic. The area is disease-ridden. Rats and dogs search alongside the scavengers. Desperation to fill their bags means fights often break out and every year there are a number of deaths. UNICEF-sponsored projects are helping to remove children from the dump and get them back to education.

# Learning checklist

| Red: **I don't know this.** Orange: **I need to study this again.** Green: **Good to go!** | ● | ● | ● |
|---|---|---|---|
| I can recognise the need to live in a sustainable way. | | | |
| I appreciate the need to manage waste responsibly. | | | |
| I can distinguish between organic and inorganic waste and I can give examples of both. | | | |
| I can explain what is meant by the EU waste hierarchy. | | | |
| I can define the terms 'biodegradable' and 'recycling'. | | | |
| I can list the items of household waste that can be recycled and outline the advantages. | | | |
| I can outline some ways to be more energy efficient. | | | |
| I know how to conserve water. | | | |
| I can outline some ways that consumers can help the environment when shopping, at home and in their locality. | | | |
| I can name an agency involved with raising awareness about sustainability and the environment. | | | |

**The topic I most enjoyed in this chapter:** _____

**The topic I would like to learn more about:** _____

# Strand 2 review
## In this strand, you learned about:

* The family
* Health and wellbeing
* The consumer
* Decision-making
* Design in the home
* Technology in the home
* Sustainable and responsible living

Look back over the topics covered in Strand 2. On the table below, identify (tick) which of the skills you have used as you worked through Strand 2 **Responsible family living**.

### Managing myself
- I know more about myself. ○
- I made considered decisions. ○
- I set and achieved goals. ○
- I reflected on my learning. ○
- I made use of technology in my learning. ○

### Staying well
- I am more aware of being healthy and active. ○
- I am social. ○
- I feel safe. ○
- I am spiritual. ○
- I feel confident. ○
- I feel positive about what I learned. ○
- I am responsible, safe and ethical in using digital technology. ○

### Managing information and thinking
- I am curious. ○
- I gathered and analysed information. ○
- I thought creatively and critically. ○
- I reflected on and evaluated my learning. ○
- I used digital technology to access, manage and share information. ○

### 1,2,3... Being numerate
- I expressed ideas mathematically. ○
- I estimated, predicted and calculated. ○
- I was interested in problem-solving. ○
- I saw patterns, trends and relationships. ○
- I gathered, analysed and presented data. ○
- I used digital technology to develop numeracy skills and understanding. ○

### Being creative
- I used my imagination. ○
- I explored options and alternatives. ○
- I put ideas into action. ○
- I learned in a creative way. ○
- I was creative with digital technology. ○

### Working with others
- I developed good relationships. ○
- I dealt with conflict. ○
- I co-operated with others while respecting difference. ○
- I helped make the world a better place. ○
- I learned with others. ○
- I worked with others using digital technology. ○

### Communicating
- I used language. ○
- I used numbers. ○
- I listened to my classmates. ○
- I expressed myself. ○
- I performed/presented. ○
- I had a discussion/debate. ○
- I used technology to communicate. ○

### Being literate
- I developed my language skills. ○
- I enjoyed words and language. ○
- I wrote for different purposes. ○
- I expressed my ideas clearly and accurately. ○
- I developed my spoken language. ○
- I read and wrote in different ways. ○

## Textiles in the home

1. Explain what is meant by textiles.

   _materials that are natural or synthetic or a combination of both._

2. Suggest four uses of textiles in the home:

   **(a)** _curtains_

   **(b)** _towels_

   **(c)** _blankets_

   **(d)** _clothing_

3. **(a)** Explain what is meant by upholstery.

   _Fabric and filling of interior furnishings._

   **(b)** Outline one precaution to reduce fire risk in upholstered furniture.

   _flame retardant finishes on the outside of fabric, so that it does not catch fire easily._

4. Illustrate a fire safety label found on upholstered furniture (see p. 285 of your textbook).

   RESISTANT

5. Explain what is meant by the term 'the properties of textiles'.

   _The characteristics - how does it feel_

6. Suggest the properties considered to be important in each of the following.

   **(a)** Sportswear: _Light, washable, stretchy_

   **(b)** Baby clothes: _Soft, washable, comfortable_

**7.** Outline two functions of soft furnishings.

(a) _give character and style to a room_

(b) _add warmth and comfort to the home_

**8.** Identify three factors that should be considered when choosing textiles for the home.

(a) _cost_

(b) _colour, pattern and style_

(c) _durability_

**9.** Explain one reason why it is important to choose sustainable textiles.

_because of the impact on the environment._

**10.** Suggest three factors to consider when choosing curtains for a living room.

(a) _how easy is it to clean?_    (b) _cost_    (c) _colour, pattern and style_

**11.** Complete the following table on curtains.

| Functions | Desirable properties |
|---|---|
| insulating ~~add styen~~ stain resistant strong | style pattern ~~colour~~ |

**12.** Use the information on the care label to help answer the following questions (see Chapter 29 Textile care).

> **Healy's Curtains**
>
> 50% COTTON
> 50% POLYESTER
> LENGTH: 180 CM
> WIDTH: 140 CM
> MADE IN IRELAND

(a) What textiles are these curtains made of? _cotton and polyester_

(b) What term is used to describe a mixture of fabrics? _a blend_

(c) At what temperature would you wash these curtains? _40°_

(d) What instructions are given on ironing the curtains? _no ironing_

(e) Can these curtains be bleached? _no_

**13.** Suggest three properties of carpets that would make it a suitable floor covering for a bedroom.

(a) _resilient_ (b) _Stain resistant_ (c) _fire resistant_

**14.** Indicate in the table below whether each of the following fibres is natural or man-made.

| Fibre | Natural | Man-made |
|-------|---------|----------|
| Wool | ✓ | ○ |
| Polyester | ○ | ○ |
| Cotton | ✓ | ○ |
| Acrylic | ○ | ✓ |
| Nylon | ○ | ○ |
| Silk | ✓ | ○ |

**15.** Draw symbols for:

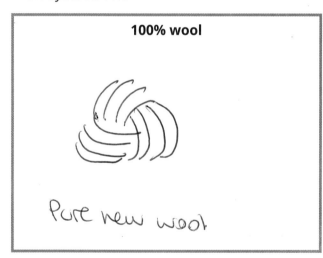

100% wool

Pure new wool

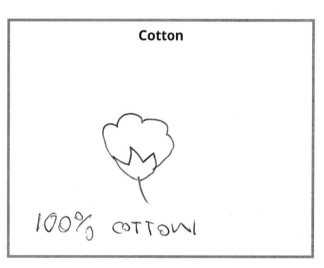

Cotton

100% COTTON

# Clothing

**1.** Explain the following terms.

(a) Fashion: _what is in style or in vogue._

(b) Fashion fad: _what is popular for a short period of time._

(c) Fashion trend: _what is popular during a decade._

**2.** Suggest four factors that influence fashion trends.

(a) _Designer's ideas_

(b) _Technology_

(c) _World events_

(d) _Celebrities_

3. Explain the following terms.

    **(a)** Couturier: _a seamstress or dressmaker_

    **(b)** Haute couture: _high fashion, made to measure, original_

    **(c)** Prêt-à-porter: _mass produced, ready to wear_

4. Outline one way that technology has influenced fashion trends.

    _Celebrities may post pictures of themselves on social media, and people might decide to wear clothes similar to theirs._

5. Name one public figure or celebrity and explain how you feel they have influenced fashion.

    **(a)** Name: _Paris Hilton_

    **(b)** How have they influenced fashion? _She is a very famous celebrity and model who many people know, and she influences fashion trends because of her modelling career._

6. State four functions of clothing.

    **(a)** _privacy_     **(b)** _fashion_

    **(c)** _warmth_     **(d)** _keep dry_

7. Identify four factors that would influence you when choosing (a) sportswear and (b) clothes for a night out.

| Sportwear | Clothes for a night out |
| --- | --- |
| cost | cost |
| washable | drapes well |
| light | easy to clean |
| cool | smooth |

8. Draw two T-shirts and illustrate how you might personalise them.

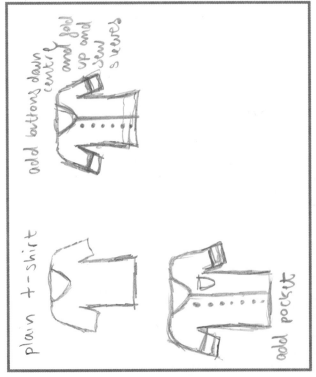

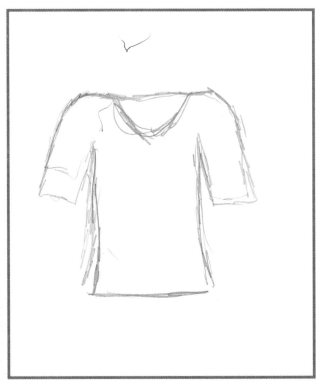

**9.** Sketch and describe a sports top you would make for your PE class.

_____
_____
_____
_____
_____
_____
_____
_____

**10. (a)** Suggest three guidelines that should be followed by teenagers when buying clothes.

**(i)** _____

**(ii)** _____

**(iii)** _____

**(b)** Name, sketch and describe an item of clothing that is popular among teenagers.

Name: _____

Description: _____

_____

_____

_____

_____

_____

**11.** What are accessories? List three accessories that are currently in fashion.

**(a)** _hairbands_

**(b)** _____

**(c)** _hairties_

**(d)** _____

**12.** Suggest two reasons why accessories are used in fashion.

**(a)** _to complete a look/outfit_

**(b)** _add interest_

**13.** Giving one example in each case, explain how the following influence textile design.

**(a)** Colour: _____

**(b)** Pattern: _____

**14.** Explain how each of the following can affect the appearance of a shirt.

(a) Vertical lines: _____

(b) Horizontal lines: _____

# Over to you

**1.** In the word search, find and define six fashion terms.

| A | J | A | Y | X | I | X | A | U | S | A | B | S | Z | I |
|---|---|---|---|---|---|---|---|---|---|---|---|---|---|---|
| F | C | C | O | R | D | T | N | H | B | S | V | B | V | D |
| Q | O | C | L | Z | F | V | F | O | M | D | K | Q | E | H |
| J | T | W | E | H | J | D | A | G | P | N | H | B | O | M |
| K | S | Z | G | S | B | D | T | X | M | E | S | Q | N | Z |
| S | T | M | L | I | S | C | A | M | J | R | F | L | D | C |
| Y | Y | D | O | K | V | O | C | L | T | T | E | X | O | S |
| C | O | N | Z | D | E | U | R | S | Q | T | V | U | C | Z |
| U | O | P | Q | P | K | T | R | I | U | F | T | U | G | G |
| R | B | F | J | V | T | U | B | A | E | U | A | K | I | P |
| W | E | M | Z | D | Y | R | H | J | R | S | C | D | U | B |
| S | F | T | J | C | Q | I | N | E | L | F | M | Q | L | F |
| S | O | U | R | Z | K | E | N | O | I | H | S | A | F | W |
| P | R | E | T | O | D | R | L | N | B | F | R | W | J | O |
| B | Y | T | R | Z | P | J | A | O | R | H | F | F | H | F |

(a) Term: _____ Definition: _____

(b) Term: _____ Definition: _____

(c) Term: _____ Definition: _____

(d) Term: _____ Definition: _____

(e) Term: _____ Definition: _____

(f) Term: _____ Definition: _____

**2.** Research current fashion trends online and using magazines. Make a collage of the fashions that appeal to you and display them in the classroom.

# Learning checklist

**Red: I don't know this. Orange: I need to study this again. Green: Good to go!**  ● ● ●

| | Red | Orange | Green |
|---|---|---|---|
| I can state some uses of textiles in the home. | | | |
| I can explain what is meant by upholstery. | | | |
| I appreciate the importance of fire safety for upholstered furniture. | | | |
| I understand what is meant by the properties and characteristics of a textile and I can list some characteristics. | | | |
| I know what is meant by soft furnishings and I can explain the function of soft furnishings. | | | |
| I can state some examples of natural and man-made fibres. | | | |
| I can suggest some properties and uses of some commonly used fabrics and I can appreciate the need to choose sustainable textiles. | | | |
| I can make considered decisions when choosing household textiles. | | | |
| I can explain what is meant by fashion trends and fashion fads. | | | |
| I can outline the effects of the fashion industry, public figures, technology and world events on fashion trends. | | | |
| I can suggest reasons why we need clothing. | | | |
| I can think creatively and critically about clothing choices. | | | |
| I can explain what accessories are and I can give examples. | | | |
| I can describe how design features and principles influence fashion. | | | |

**The topic I most enjoyed in this chapter:** _____

**The topic I would like to learn more about:** _____

# 26 Sewing skills

## Sewing equipment

1. List six pieces of sewing equipment.

    (a) _____  (b) _____  (c) _____

    (d) _____  (e) _____  (f) _____

2. Identify the following pieces of sewing equipment and explain their uses.

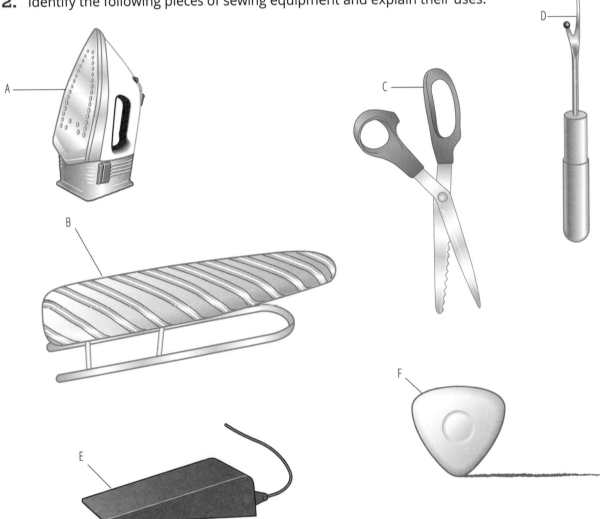

A. _____

B. _____

C. _____

D. _____

E. _____

F. _____

# Hand stitches

**1.** Suggest two guidelines for hand stitching.

(a) _____

(b) _____

**2.** Identify four hand stitches. Give a use for each.

| Hand stitch | Use |
|---|---|
|  |  |
|  |  |
|  |  |
|  |  |

**3.** Identify the stitches in the following diagrams and state one use for each stitch.

A        B        C

| Stitch | Use |
|---|---|
| A. |  |
| B. |  |
| C. |  |

**4.** Name a stitch suitable for finishing the hem of a dress. _____

**5.** Indicate if the following statements are true or false.

| Tacking is: | True | False |
|---|---|---|
| A secure straight stitch used instead of machining. | ○ | ○ |
| A temporary stitch used to hold two pieces of fabric together. | ○ | ○ |
| A permanent stitch used on the hem of clothes. | ○ | ○ |
| A stitch started with a knot in the thread. | ○ | ○ |

**6.** Identify the following stitches and suggest a use for each.

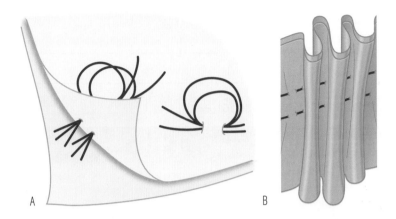

A                                                                    B

| Stitch | Use |
|--------|-----|
| A. | |
| B. | |

# The sewing machine

**1.** The sewing machine is a useful resource. Label the following diagram.

A. _____

B. _____

C. _____

D. _____

E. _____

F. _____

G. _____

H. _____

I. _____

J. _____

K. _____

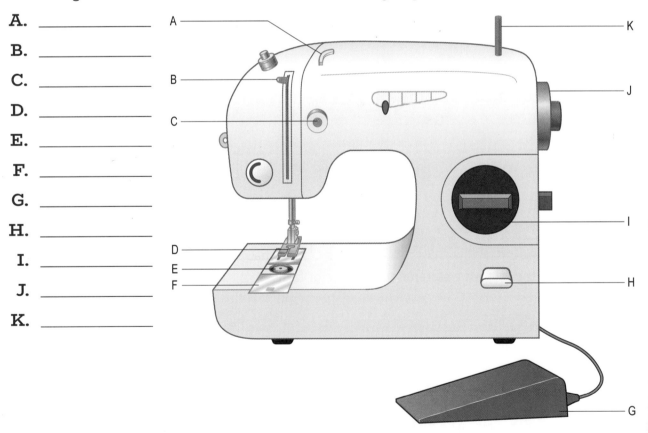

**2.** Show the correct way to thread a sewing machine on the diagram above.

3. Complete the functions of the following parts of the sewing machine.

| Part | Function |
|---|---|
| Presser foot | |
| Tension screw | |
| Foot pedal | |
| Bobbin case | |
| Pattern selector | |

4. When choosing a sewing machine what should you consider?

(a) _____

(b) _____

(c) _____

(d) _____

5. Complete the four machine stitches. Give a use for each.

| Machine stitch | Use |
|---|---|
| | |
| | |
| | |
| | |

6. Suggest a machine stitch suitable for the following.

(a) Appliqué: _____

(b) Turning up a hem: _____

7. State four guidelines to follow when using a sewing machine.

(a) _____

(b) _____

(c) _____

(d) _____

8. Explain why it is important to test machine stitching on a spare piece of fabric.

_____

9. List two points on the care of a sewing machine.

(a) _____   (b) _____

**10.** Identify two machine faults. Give two possible causes of each.

| Fault | Possible causes |
|---|---|
|  |  |
|  |  |

**11. (a)** Suggest two ways to neaten/finish a flat seam.

(i) _____ (ii) _____

**(b)** Why is it necessary to neaten a seam? _____

**12.** From the diagram, identify:

**(a)** The type of seam _____

**(b)** The seam finish used _____

# Sewing fabrics

**1.** State two guidelines to follow when buying fabrics.

**(a)** _____

**(b)** _____

**2.** Explain the following terms.

**(a)** Nap: _____

**(b)** One-way design: _____

**3.** Define the following terms.

**(a)** Warp threads/selvage: _____

**(b)** Weft threads: _____

**4.** Explain the following terms.

**(a)** Bias: _____

**(b)** Straight grain: _____

**5.** Suggest one use for:

**(a)** Bias strips _____

**(b)** Tailor's chalk _____

**6.** Give two guidelines for cutting out fabric.

**(a)** _____

**(b)** _____

**7.** Suggest two ways to transfer pattern markings from the paper pattern to the fabric.

**(a)** _____

**(b)** _____

# Over to you 👉

1.  Visit a sewing machine supplier or research online:

    (a) The cost of three different sewing machines

    (b) The features of each machine

    (c) The attachments included

    (d) The guarantee included

2.  Make charts of (a) a labelled diagram of a sewing machine and (b) hand stitches. Display the charts on the wall of the Home Economics room.

# Learning checklist

| Red: I don't know this. Orange: I need to study this again. Green: Good to go! | 🔴 | 🔘 | 🔘 |
|---|---|---|---|
| I can label the parts of a sewing machine. | | | |
| I can list points to consider when choosing a sewing machine. | | | |
| I can name different machine stitches and I can give their uses. | | | |
| I can apply my knowledge of how to care for a sewing machine, thread it and use it safely. | | | |
| I can list faults that might occur and I can give the reasons for the faults. | | | |
| I can outline the basic equipment necessary for sewing. | | | |
| I can identify the basic hand stitches and I can list a use for each. | | | |
| I can demonstrate basic hand- and machine-sewing techniques. | | | |
| I can explain what a flat seam is, and I know how to make and neaten the seam. | | | |
| I can outline points to consider when buying fabric. | | | |
| I can explain what is meant by nap, one-way design, warp/selvage, weft and bias. | | | |
| I can describe how to cut out fabric correctly and transfer pattern markings onto fabric. | | | |
| I can set and achieve personal goals in relation to my practical sewing skills. | | | |

**The topic I most enjoyed in this chapter:** _____

**The topic I would like to learn more about:** _____

# 27 Fabric embellishment

1. Explain the term 'fabric embellishment'. _adding decoration to improve the appearance_

2. Suggest two reasons why textile work is regarded as therapeutic.
   (a) _it can be very relaxing_
   (b) _it lets us worry less about our problems_

3. State two items of clothing that could be embellished giving an example in each case.
   (a) _jeans: patchwork or embroidery_
   (b) _a shirt: embroidery designs_

4. Name two nousehold items that could be embellished giving an example in each case.
   (a) _pillow - patchwork, embroidery_
   (b) _blanket - embroidery    or adding features e.g buttons_

5. Identify two advantages of embellishing fabrics.
   (a) _personalises the fabric_
   (b) _can make it more attractive_

6. Name and describe how to implement one method of embellishment.
   _Embroidery - stitching decorative features on textiles. Can be done by machine or by hand_

7. Give two differences between sewing thread and embroidery thread.
   (a) _Embroidery thread is thicker_
   (b) _Embroidery thread is made with a soft texture while sewing thread is strong._

8. What type of needle is usually used for embroidery? Explain why.
   _A crewel needle (with a large eye) is used for embroidery so that the thread can fit._

9. Name the two embroidery stitches shown below and suggest a use for each.
   A. _satin stitch_
   B. _chain stitch_

A

B

**10.** Explain the following terms.

    **(a)** Dyeing: _____

    **(b)** Printing: _____

**11.** What is the function of a mordant when dyeing fabric?

_____

**12.** State two methods of dyeing.

    **(a)** _____     **(b)** _____

**13.** State two methods of printing.

    **(a)** _____     **(b)** _____

**14.** Identify the following methods of embellishment.

_____    _____    _____

_____    _____    _____

**15.** Illustrate and describe the embellishment you would add to a plain pillowcase.

_____

_____

_____

_____

# Over to you

1. Collect pictures of different methods of embellishing fabrics. Make a collage and display it in the Home Economics room.

2. Research different techniques for embellishing fabrics. Practise three different methods and stick samples into your folder.

3. Solve the following anagrams of types of fabric embellishment.

| | |
|---|---|
| nitngirp | |
| yedgni | |
| bemridorey | |
| froingruw | |
| kisngcom | |
| taplegin | |
| gipinp | |
| bindeag | |
| furfles | |
| kropawcht | |

# Learning checklist

| Red: **I don't know this.** Orange: **I need to study this again.** Green: **Good to go!** | ● | ● | ● |
|---|---|---|---|
| I can explain what is meant by fabric embellishment. | | | |
| I can suggest different methods used to embellish textiles. | | | |
| I can identify different embroidery stitches and suggest a use for each. | | | |
| I can explain the difference between dyeing and printing fabric. | | | |
| I can apply some fabric embellishment techniques. | | | |
| I appreciate the therapeutic and leisure role of participating in textile work. | | | |

**The topic I most enjoyed in this chapter:** _____

**The topic I would like to learn more about:** _____

# Sustainability in textiles

1. State three ecological problems associated with the textile industry.

   (a) _clothes not recycled_

   (b) _gases from factories_

   (c) _plastics thrown away in clothes._

2. Suggest three ethical issues associated with the production of textiles.

   (a) _child labour_

   (b) _unfair wages for workers_

   (c) _animal cruelty_

3. State one advantage in each case.

   (a) Giving your old clothes to your younger brother or sister: ~~reusing~~ _reusing_

   (b) Swapping clothes with your friends: _not throwing them away_

   (c) Donating your clothes to charity: _gives someone else a chance to buy them_

   (d) Upcycling and reusing your old clothes: _gives old clothes a new lease of life_

4. Suggest old textile items you could use to make the following items.

   (a) Cleaning cloths: _pillowcase, blanket or cushion cover_

   (b) Pet blanket: _towel_

   (c) Patchwork cushion: _small blanket or duvet cover_

   (d) Shopping bag: _pillowcase_

5. Indicate whether each statement is true or false.

| Statement | True | False |
|---|---|---|
| Most textile waste is recycled. | ○ | ✓ |
| Recycling reduces the amount of chemicals used to manufacture new textiles. | ✓ | ○ |
| Recycling uses more energy than processing fabrics from raw materials. | ○ | ✓ |
| Synthetic materials decompose in landfill sites. | ○ | ✓ |

6. Name three products that are made from recycled materials.

   (a) _paper notebooks_ (b) _backpacks_ (c) _shopping bags_

**7.** Explain what is meant by upcycling.

*changing an item to update it or for another purpose*

**8.** Give two examples of upcycling.

(a) *changing a dress into a top or skirt*

(b) *a knitted jumper into a cushion*

**9.** Suggest two advantages of upcycling.

(a) *reduces waste*

(b) *cost effective*

# Over to you 👉

**1.** Complete the crossword about the textile industry.

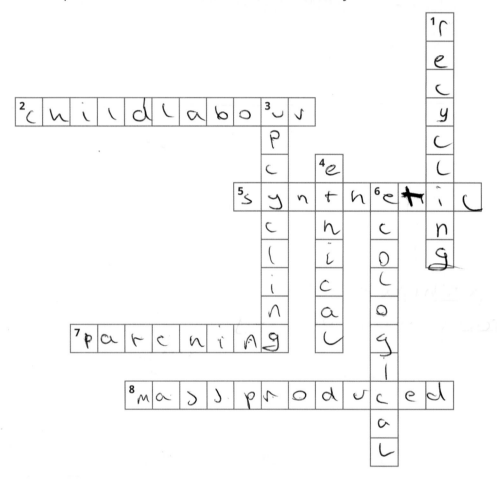

## Across

**2.** Children working in unsafe conditions

**5.** Another name for man-made fibres

**7.** A method of repairing fabric

**8.** When clothing is produced in large amounts

## Down

**1.** Reusing or reprocessing textiles

**3.** Creative reuse

**4.** Issues that are concerned with a sense of right or wrong

**6.** Issues that affect the environment

**2.** Research online advertisements for the prevention of child labour. Debate the effectiveness of these advertisements in influencing people's choice of textiles.

# Learning checklist

| Red: I don't know this. Orange: I need to study this again. Green: Good to go! | ● | ● | ● |
|---|---|---|---|
| I understand some environmental problems caused by the textile industry. | | | |
| I can list some ethical problems associated with the production of textiles. | | | |
| I can apply methods of repairing textiles and I can list advantages of mending clothes. | | | |
| I can describe how to mend a textile item by darning or patching it. | | | |
| I can define textile recycling. | | | |
| I can outline the benefits of recycling textiles. | | | |
| I can identify some uses of recycled textiles. | | | |
| I can describe what is meant by upcycling and I can describe some creative upcycling ideas. | | | |
| I can appreciate the value of repairing, reusing, repurposing and upcycling textiles. | | | |
| I can use my imagination to explore ideas for turning waste textiles into useful or decorative items. | | | |
| I can think creatively and critically about textile sustainability. | | | |

**The topic I most enjoyed in this chapter:** _____

**The topic I would like to learn more about:** _____

# 29 Textile care

1. Suggest three guidelines for the care of clothing.

   (a) keep them clean - wash at correct temperature

   (b) fold / hang when not worn

   (c) repair when damaged

2. Explain the following symbols, which appeared on the care label of a shirt, by giving the instructions in writing.

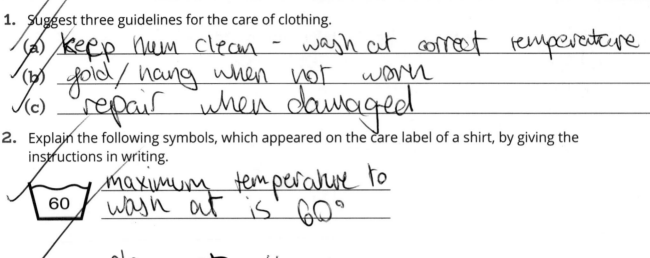

   maximum temperature to wash at is 60°

   do not bleach

   iron at medium temperature

   do tumble dry

3. The following instructions appeared on the label of a uniform jumper that is an acrylic wool blend.

   ◆ Dry clean or hand wash only     ◆ Warm iron

   ◆ Do not bleach     ◆ Dry flat

   Draw the symbols for the instructions.

   dry flat

   hand wash only

   do not bleach

   warm iron

   dry clean

**4.** Design care labels for the following: (a) a silk scarf (b) a cotton shirt.

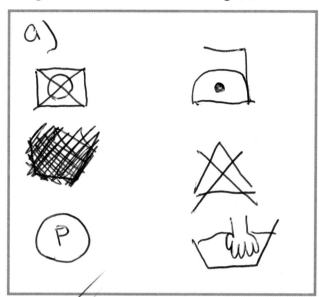

**5.** Match the symbol with the appropriate instruction.

   (i)  Bleach can be used _G_

   (ii)  Maximum wash _E_

   (iii)  Line dry _D_

   (iv)  Do not tumble dry _A_

   (v)  Cool iron _F_

   (vi)  Dry cleaning instructions _H_

   (vii)  Hand wash only _B_

   (viii)  Hot iron _C_

  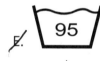   

**6.** State two guidelines for the care of delicate fabrics.

(a) dry clean – no tumble drying if the fabric is delicate

(b) no bleaching

**7.** Suggest a way to remove the following stains.

(a) Ink: ~~~~ apply hand sanitiser and wash

(b) Gravy: use heavy duty ~~~~ liquid detergent

(c) Chewing gum: put ~~~~ item in the freezer

**8.** State two safety guidelines for using commercial stain removers.

(a) _____

(b) _____

**9. (a)** Name and state the function of three chemicals found in detergents.

(i) bleach - removes stain

(ii) flouroscent - ~~b~~ ~~brighten~~ brightens colour

(iii) enzymes - break down food stains

**(b)** Suggest one way to prevent the colour of a garment from fading when it is being washed.

~~put in colder~~ ~~flouroscent to whiten the~~ ~~colour~~ reduce temperature

**10.** Explain the following terms.

**(a)** Biological detergents: have enzymes

**(b)** Eco-friendly detergents: have less chemicals

**11.** Fill in the functions of detergents and conditioners.

| Detergents | Conditioners |
|---|---|
| clean | softens clothes |
| ~~scrub~~ ~~breaks down stains~~ remove stains, | reduces static |
| scent / perfume | scent / perfume |

**12.** Suggest three ways to save energy and water when using a washing machine.

(a) use full loads

(b) ~~don't put in the wash for~~ ~~shorter wash cycle~~ shorter wash

(c) reduce temperature as much as possible

**13.** Explain why line drying is best for drying clothes and household textiles.

enviromentally friendly as it is drying naturally

**14.** Suggest two guidelines on how to iron clothes successfully.

(a) follow care label for ironing temperature

(b) iron flat

**15.** Suggest one advantage of using a steam iron when ironing clothes.

_____

_____

_____

# Over to you 👉

1. Suggest one reason for each of the following:

   **(a)** Check the care label before washing clothes. _____

   **(b)** Empty all the pockets before washing. _____

   **(c)** Close buttons and zips before washing. _____

   **(d)** Wash delicate fabrics separately, by hand. _____

   **(e)** Treat a stain as soon as it happens. _____

   **(f)** Always test stain removers on an unseen part of the fabric first. _____

   _____

   **(g)** Carefully follow the instructions on commercial stain removers. _____

   _____

   **(h)** Use stain removers in a ventilated room. _____

   _____

   **(i)** Keep detergents away from young children. _____

   **(j)** Only wash when you have a full load. _____

   **(k)** Use eco-friendly detergents and methods of stain removal where possible. _____

   _____

   **(l)** Choose laundry products with biodegradable or refillable packaging. _____

   **(m)** Select the correct heat setting when ironing. _____

   **(n)** Iron some fabrics on the wrong side. _____

   **(o)** Do not iron over buttons or zips. _____

   **(p)** Dry clothes outside when possible. _____

   **(q)** Avoid using the tumble dryer. _____

2. Look up the textile terms on pp. 329–30 of your textbook and explain each of the terms.

   **(a)** Appliqué: _____

   **(b)** Dart: _____

   **(c)** Gathering: _____

   **(d)** Raw edge: _____

3. Apply your knowledge of textile care by:

   **(a)** Laundering a delicate item, e.g. a scarf

   **(b)** Sorting, washing and drying a full load of laundry

   **(c)** Ironing a shirt

# Learning checklist

| Red: I don't know this. Orange: I need to study this again. Green: Good to go! | ● | ● | ● |
|---|---|---|---|
| I can explain how to care for clothing. | | | |
| I can identify the different symbols for fabric care and I can explain what each means. | | | |
| I can prepare clothing for washing and I can use a washing machine. | | | |
| I can describe how to launder delicate fabrics. | | | |
| I can list precautions to follow when using commercial stain removers. | | | |
| I can outline ways to remove common stains. | | | |
| I can list some ingredients found in detergents. | | | |
| I appreciate the advantages of choosing eco-friendly detergents. | | | |
| I can list functions of detergents and fabric conditioners. | | | |
| I can name some eco-friendly stain removers. | | | |
| I can outline how clothing is dried and ironed. | | | |
| I can evaluate textile care procedures used in the home in terms of their impact on the environment. | | | |
| I can describe some ways of saving water and energy when washing and drying textiles. | | | |

**The topic I most enjoyed in this chapter:** _____

**The topic I would like to learn more about:** _____

Select possible solutions for each of the following briefs.

| Brief | Possible solutions |
|---|---|
| Make a textile item for an individual. | |
| Make a textile item for the home. | |
| Recycle or upcycle a textile item for an individual. | |
| Recycle or upcycle a textile item for the home. | |

# Strand 3 review
## In this strand, you learned about:

- Textile trends and choices
- Sewing skills
- Fabric embellishment
- Sustainability in textiles
- Textile care

Look back over the topics covered in Strand 3. On the table below, identify (tick) which of the skills you have used as you worked through Strand 3 **Textiles and craft**.

| Managing myself | Staying well | Managing information and thinking | 1,2,3... Being numerate |
|---|---|---|---|
| I know more about myself. ◯ | I am more aware of being healthy and active. ◯ | I am curious. ◯ | I expressed ideas mathematically. ◯ |
| I made considered decisions. ◯ | I am social. ◯ | I gathered and analysed information. ◯ | I estimated, predicted and calculated. ◯ |
| I set and achieved goals. ◯ | I feel safe. ◯ | I thought creatively and critically. ◯ | I was interested in problem-solving. ◯ |
| I reflected on my learning. ◯ | I am spiritual. ◯ | I reflected on and evaluated my learning. ◯ | I saw patterns, trends and relationships. ◯ |
| I made use of technology in my learning. ◯ | I feel confident. ◯ | I used digital technology to access, manage and share information. ◯ | I gathered, analysed and presented data. ◯ |
| | I feel positive about what I learned. ◯ | | I used digital technology to develop numeracy skills and understanding. ◯ |
| | I am responsible, safe and ethical in using digital technology. ◯ | | |

| Being creative | Working with others | Communicating | abc Being literate |
|---|---|---|---|
| I used my imagination. ◯ | I developed good relationships. ◯ | I used language. ◯ | I developed my language skills. ◯ |
| I explored options and alternatives. ◯ | I dealt with conflict. ◯ | I used numbers. ◯ | I enjoyed words and language. ◯ |
| I put ideas into action. ◯ | I co-operated with others while respecting difference. ◯ | I listened to my classmates. ◯ | I wrote for different purposes. ◯ |
| I learned in a creative way. ◯ | I helped make the world a better place. ◯ | I expressed myself. ◯ | I expressed my ideas clearly and accurately. ◯ |
| I was creative with digital technology. ◯ | I learned with others. ◯ | I performed/presented. ◯ | I developed my spoken language. ◯ |
| | I worked with others using digital technology. ◯ | I had a discussion/debate. ◯ | I read and wrote in different ways. ◯ |
| | | I used technology to communicate. ◯ | |